Happy 15th Birthday
Florida - Nov. 1977

how to
break
90/80/par

Cliff McAdams

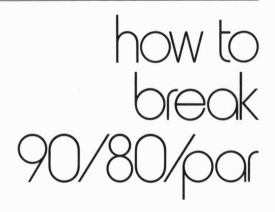

how to
break
90/80/par

WINCHESTER PRESS

Library of Congress Catalog Card Number: 73-75667
ISBN: 0-87691-101-7

Published by Winchester Press
460 Park Avenue, New York 10022

Printed in the United States of America

Preface

It's often stated that you can't learn golf from books, and superficially, at least, the statement is true. The vast majority of golfers who have won acclaim owe their success to countless hours of instruction, endless practice sessions, and a powerful desire to succeed, not to reading golf books. Still, books can be valuable adjuncts to instruction and practice, once the player has progressed enough to understand written theory and to be able to put it into practice.

It would be foolish to deny, however, that a great many books of golf instruction have confused their readers, sometimes with verbiage and sometimes with facts—or rather, too many facts. (Sometimes, too, written instruction has appeared *sans* facts.) A common reason is lack of attention to the fact that every player is a unique individual. Some grasp quickly and some do not, some are talented and some are not, and it's foolish to think that all can progress in the same way or at the same pace.

Put another way, players who are only starting to learn to play golf should not be burdened by technical matter that might be appropriate for advanced players, and conversely, good players should not be burdened with the kind of basic matter needed by beginners.

How to Break 90/80/Par is meant for players of all types —those who are presently shooting in the 90s, those who are striving to reach the 70s, and those within striking distance of par. But to keep from boring the good player or puzzling the beginner, each chapter in the book has been written specifically for players at a certain level, and the book is divided into three sections. In the first section the most fundamental subjects are thoroughly explained. In "How to Break 80," intermediate subjects are detailed. And in "How to Break Par" you will find some of the advanced considerations the near-scratch player must reckon with.

Except for my introductory chapter for each section, the chapters in this book were written by outstanding professionals, outstanding teachers. Several have reached the pinnacle of competitive success, and others have achieved that rare status of "teacher of teachers." And all have been winners in tournament play.

Each writer's method of teaching the game melds with the others'. Their methods are harmonious; their ideas blend. Thus a player who has absorbed the instruction of an early chapter can build on that knowledge and integrate it with advice from later chapters.

The many photographs are an important adjunct to the text. They should be studied carefully, for they explain better than words can many of the key points about the game. They both supplement and clarify the text.

One can learn golf from a book, of course—at least one can learn enough to improve. We think you'll agree, after reading the following chapters and putting their precepts into practice on the course.

Contents

HOW TO BREAK 90

HOW TO BREAK 80

HOW TO BREAK PAR

part 1

how to
break
90

escaping from dufferdom

About 80 percent of all golfers have never broken 90. This is a shame, for if you are of sound limb and have a modicum of desire, it really shouldn't prove all that difficult. In fact, if you can just hit the ball reasonably straight and not very far, there's no reason for you to have to hit it more than 89 times a round. "Straight" is the magic word for the 90 shooter. Simply keeping the ball in play—avoiding penalty strokes and double bogies—is the main key to lower scores, for bogey golf is really all you need. Consider, if you will, that on a par-72 course you can bogey seventeen of the eighteen holes and still break 90. If you can hit the ball straight, even if your "big hit" is only 180 yards, shooting in the high 80s should be a cinch. A drive of 180 yards in the fairway will put you within reach of most par 4s with your second shot, and get you home on the average par 3. On longer par 3s, you'll still be in position for an easy lay-up and a possible one-putt green. On long par 4s which you can't reach in two shots, the same situation will apply. Two straight blows of medium length

3

put you in position for an easy pitch to the pin, while two long shots that are wild will put you in deep trouble.

What do you need to hit the ball straight? Nothing fancier than basic fundamentals! It's that simple. Using the proper grip and stance will go a long way toward developing a repeating swing that will permit you to hit the ball squarely and consistently. But any weakness in these two key fundamentals will invite all kinds of swing errors.

For example, a weak grip will accentuate your slice, if you have one. (A weak grip is one in which the hands are too far to the left on the shaft.) This grip tends to leave the clubface open at impact, causing it to strike the ball an oblique blow. With a weak grip, the average slicer will intuitively aim more and more to the left of his target to accommodate the banana curves on his shots. Soon he loses all sense of alignment and direction.

A grip that is fundamentally sound not only makes for consistent clubface alignment at impact, but allows the hands and wrists to hinge freely for greater clubhead speed. Hitting the ball straight is the principal dividend. Hitting it farther is a bonus.

Your stance will greatly influence your swing plane, and the swing plane will affect the flight of the ball. Your height and body build will determine how closely your stance can follow the accepted "norm" or your favorite golf star, be he Jack Nicklaus, Lee Trevino, or George Archer. So, don't imitate your golfing idol unless you have a similar physique.

Other swing ingredients are important, of course, and it goes without saying that the swing is not a static thing, but a continuum of movement. Some of these other factors are covered on ensuing pages, but we must emphasize that a consistent swing path that propels the ball straight is virtually impossible without a good grip and stance.

Inconsistency is the principal plague of most high-handicappers. Uncertainty destroys confidence and induces tension, and tension ruins rhythm and timing. If you can wallop the ball 275 yards off the tee but don't know where it's going, what good is the distance? A ball in the deep rough or out of bounds is too severe a penalty to pay. A few penalty strokes for miscued shots will completely demoralize the average player. *Straight* pays off; *crooked* costs strokes.

Golf is a game in which it's disastrous to defy fundamentals, especially for the weekend player. Unless you devote every waking hour to golf, there is no way you can hit the ball consistently straight with a "novelty" swing. If your grip and stance tend to invert the clubhead at address or impact, opening it, you're off to a bad start. If you open or close the clubface abruptly during the swing—in spite of the proper grip and stance—your error can easily be spotted and corrected.

So in golf, as in any other kind of learning, the basics must come first. A sound grip and correct stance make the fundamentals of the actual swing infinitely easier to learn. Once you have a sound, grooved swing, the way is open for acquiring the finesse good scoring demands. The woods and long irons are hit with virtually the same swing, and the shorter irons then come easier. So let's see how to go about establishing a sound grip and stance.

grip and stance

2

by Henry Williams

It's impossible to overemphasize the importance of the grip. The grip directly affects the position of your clubhead throughout your swing and during impact. A faulty grip that won't allow the hands and wrists to work to their best anatomical advantage can deter you from ever playing good golf consistently.

The grip is the golfer's key to accurate golf. It is the focal point, the single contact the body has with the clubhead and the ball. No matter how perfect the rest of your swing is, if the grip is incorrect, it will directly affect the position of the clubhead at impact and not only cause sporadic slicing or hooking, but contribute to a great loss of distance. Sure, you can compensate and hit a few good shots with a poor grip, but you will never be consistent, which is the real key to low-handicap play.

So every golfer needs a good grip—simple enough. But what is a good grip? That question is not so simple, because each

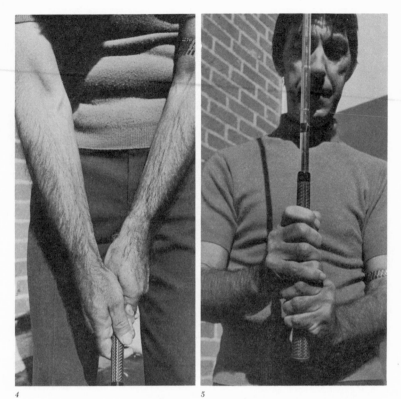

4   In the completed grip, the right thumb and forefinger are very
    close together and the thumb of the left hand is snugly in the
    "valley" of the right palm. Correct placement protects the player
    from too much righthand power.

5   The little finger of the right hand should lie across the first finger
    of the left hand or in the cavity between the left forefinger and
    middle finger, whichever seems the most comfortable.

The ten-finger grip is sometimes best for women players
or with men and boys whose hands are weak. Occasionally it is appropriate for young beginners, as it feels more natural. However, it
is best for even the very young to get used to a proper golf grip early.

A comfortable grip, of course, would seem desirable, but
comfort should not be the main criterion. You can condition yourself
to be comfortable with the most effective grip.

It is well to remember that all golfers' hands are different. No two golfers' hands are exactly the same size and shape. So it's impossible to recommend a specific grip for everyone. If your grip is questionable or you're having problems that you suspect may be associated with the grip, my advice is to see a professional. He can recommend the grip that is best for you after seeing you swing or hit some balls.

A pro can do something else for you too: you may be using the type of grip best suited to your hands, but you may not be positioning your wrists correctly. Only a good pro can teach you that.

The stance, too, is an important prerequisite to a good swing and an accurate shot. A faulty stance can produce almost the same problems as a faulty grip.

Before assuming a stance, you should check your alignment with the target. Your basic stance should be square to the target. Advanced golfers sometimes use an open or closed stance in certain situations, but everyone begins with a square stance.

When addressing the ball, your weight should be comfortably carried on the balls of your feet and your knees should be slightly flexed. The slight bending of the knees permits them to act as a cushion when you swing the club through the ball. Some beginners exaggerate this bending of the knees; it should be just an unlocking of the knees, not a half-squat.

Using the correct stance, you should have the feeling that you are "sitting down to the ball." If you don't have this feeling, check your knees and weight distribution.

When you address the ball, your arms should hang naturally from the shoulders, and the left arm should be an "extension" of the club. Make certain at address that your head is slightly behind the ball.

The feet should be spaced at about shoulder width for a full swing. However, when using more lofted clubs with shorter shafts, your feet should move closer together.

The angle of the feet is often neglected by most 90 shooters. The feet should be positioned so that they are pointing to "five minutes to one." That is, with the ball at twelve o'clock your left foot should be pointing to eleven and your right foot to one.

There is a good reason for pointing the feet in this manner. For example, if your right foot is pointing to twelve o'clock, as some golfers think is correct, it will be restricted when you pivot to the right and the other foot will choke off your follow-through.

the basic swing

by Don Fairfield

It's obvious that you're not going to acquire a fine golf swing simply by reading articles on the subject, no matter how instructive. The requisite muscle memory cannot be acquired in this manner, for example, and neither can timing and rhythm. Nonetheless, there are certain basic fundamentals that can be talked about. If you understand the theory, you may be able to use it in practice to develop an efficient swing.

A swing is efficient when the clubhead hits the ball squarely and solidly. To do that, the clubhead must make a full arc with a smooth, wide takeaway from the ball, and the golfer must make a full turn of the upper body and return the club to its original position just before it hits the ball.

Unfortunately, less attention is often paid to the initial movements of the swing than the "second part" of the swing, the downswing action of hitting the ball. But the golfer who is interested in perfecting his swing must concentrate heavily on the backswing movement.

Obviously, a good swing can result only if a good grip, stance, and posture are employed. But once you have achieved these, the next important ingredient is the backswing effort.

The order of movements on the backswing should follow this sequence: hands, arms, shoulders, hips. Of course, the time differential between these actions is slight, especially as applied to the hands, arms, and shoulders. As a matter of fact, the movements are almost together—a unified action.

It's important to remember, however, that the shoulders must always lead the hips in the turning action. Just before the hands reach the level of the hips, the shoulders, in turning, start pulling the hips. And as the hips begin to turn, the left knee starts moving to the right or is pulled to the right. It's not a complicated series of movements; in fact it's quite natural, as if you were chopping down a tree. But practice is required to perfect the action against a golf ball.

The first two feet of the takeaway action is vital. You must have a feeling that the club and left arm are moving away from the ball in a firm, unbroken line—"in one piece." But the takeaway action involves the body as well as the hands and arms. It is a movement involving the entire body. Everything moves together, except the head. The head remains steady throughout, at least to the point in the follow-through action at which the body draws it around.

The shoulders should be turned as far as they can go without undue strain. The more the shoulders are turned, the better. With a proper turn, the left shoulder will move under the chin and the back will face the target at the completion of the turn. The left arm remains straight throughout.

A common fault with many high-handicap golfers is bending the left arm. When the left arm is bent, power is forfeited and many other errors can develop.

Another fault is turning the hips too soon. The hips must be restrained until the turning of the shoulders pulls the hips around. This gives your body the coiled-spring action that results in a powerful hit.

The action of the legs is somewhat automatic. When the hips start turning, the left knee, of necessity, is pulled to the right and forward, and the left foot rolls to the right on the inside part of the sole.

18

24

The right leg action is almost nil—it should remain in relatively the same position it was at address throughout the backswing. A stable right leg will prevent the leg from collapsing and carrying the body with it.

The correct hand position at the top of the backswing has the left thumb under the shaft, supporting the weight of the club. The thumb position, of course, is largely a result of the proper grip. The back of the left hand should form a line with the left arm, without a break in the back of the left wrist.

At the top of the backswing, the clubshaft should be parallel to the target line. If it points to the right of the target line, it's incorrect and the shot will probably hook. If it points to the left, a slice will occur. The former situation results, usually, from taking the club back too much "inside" while the latter results from taking the club back too much "outside."

The downswing should start with a shifting of weight back to the left by moving the legs, hips, and shoulders. The hands should follow, and the wrists should remain in a cocked position until reaching the hitting area.

It's extremely important to have the feeling that the hands are following, rather than leading, throughout the downswing. The left arm should have a slight feeling of pulling down and through the hitting area. This is the action that produces clubhead speed.

The follow-through action should be low and complete. The clubhead should be kept on line with the target for at least four inches through the ball, and both arms should be extended as far as possible. At the finish of the swing, the hands should be high and the weight completely on the left leg, with the toe of the right foot balancing the body. The body should be facing forward.

One final reminder: the head should be held behind the ball and kept as motionless as possible during the downswing and through impact. On the follow-through action, it should turn slowly toward the target as a result of the body turn.

driving

by Bob Harrison

The ability to hit a reasonably long and accurate tee shot is a vital asset to a golfer who is striving to break 90. Achieving this distance and accuracy depends largely upon the application of sound fundamentals and a regular program of practice.

Essentials for a good drive are a good grip, stance, balance, alignment, backswing, downswing, and finish. Utilizing the theory that repetition is the best way to learn something, we'll review the highlights of a sound swing as they apply to the tee shot using a driver.

A good tee shot begins with a good grip. Having a proper grip enables a golfer to hit his tee shot accurately and with distance more consistently. A golfer should strive for a feeling of both hands working together as a single unit, with the left hand controlling the direction. The grip should be firm but not tense; it is important to place the hands on the club with no pressure, and then only enough pressure should be applied to enable you to control the club. Because the club's grip is tapered, only a slight amount of pressure is necessary.

Most teaching professionals advocate the use of the overlapping or Vardon grip. The basic overlapping grip involves holding the club lightly with the fingers of the left hand and applying pressure with the last three fingers. To fashion this grip, place your left thumb slightly to the right of center of the shaft and your right thumb left of center. The V formed by the forefinger and thumb of the left hand should point toward the right shoulder. The pressure points of the grip in the right hand should be the two middle fingers, while the little finger of the right hand overlaps the forefinger of the left hand. The angle of the V formed by the thumb and forefinger of the left hand can vary, but the right hand should match the left; the palm of the right hand and palm of the left hand should face each other. Balance the pressure in both hands for a moment, then relax your shoulders and right arm and begin your stance and alignment with your feet together at right angles to the ball.

Good golfers establish a routine in setting up their position for a tee shot. Most start the stance by placing the clubhead at an exact right angle to the intended line of flight, with the feet together at right angles. The feet should be spread slightly, the toes forming a parallel line to the line of flight. For maximum stability, the distance between your feet should be approximately the width of your shoulders. Your left foot should be pointed out slightly while the right foot should be perpendicular to the intended line of flight. Your knees, hips, and shoulders should also form a line parallel to the line of flight with the emphasis placed on the shoulders. The ball should be played on a line to the left heel at right angles to the line of flight.

For tee shots with a driver the left shoulder and hip are slightly higher than the right shoulder and hip because the right hand is lower than the left hand on the shaft. This is why most good players have the appearance of being tilted slightly to the right. Your back and shoulders should be bent forward from the hips, forming a hollow in the lower back. Flex your knees slightly, as if you were getting ready to sit down on a stool, so that your weight is toward the heels.

Stand a comfortable distance from the ball, so that you neither have to reach for it nor feel cramped. The distance from the heel of your left hand to your left thigh should be about four or five

At address, the body should be bent forward from the hips, the knees bent slightly, and the arms hanging downward to a point directly under the chin. The feet should be square with the line to the target. The left shoulder and hip should be higher than the right shoulder, and the head should be behind the ball. Weight should be evenly distributed on both feet and primarily on the heels. The ball should be played off the left heel.

inches. In order to gain a relaxed position in relation to the ball, let your arms hang downward from your shoulders to a point directly under your chin instead of out in front of you. This position helps create a more upright arc, which is desirable in most cases.

The next step is to visualize your line of flight. You must try to "see" it. If you cannot, imagine trying to hit a target with a bow and arrow while blindfolded. Have you ever lined up a putt and literally seen a line to the hole, knowing you were going to sink it even before you stroked the ball? This same feeling of confidence in your alignment should be accomplished with your tee shot. A good tee shot starts you off with a big psychological advantage.

Relaxation is vital as you prepare for your swing. Most good players waggle the clubhead over or behind the ball as they begin their backswing. This helps to relieve tension. The purpose is to keep the body moving rather than to begin the swing from a static start. Some players prefer to make a slight forward press—a movement of the hands toward the target—before starting their backswing. Whichever course you choose, practice it, work on it diligently, and make it become a routine each time you hit a tee shot.

In making your backswing, strive to make the left shoulder turn under your chin to point at the ball. Your shoulders should turn twice as much as your hips—about 90 degrees, compared with about 45 degrees for the hips. An effort should be made to brace the right knee inward to avoid possible swaying off the ball. When you prevent the right knee from laterally moving to the right, you will be able to turn the left shoulder more. The shoulder turn must be complete before the downswing is started. Your rhythm depends on a full shoulder turn.

It is important to make the backswing as much a one-piece unit as possible, with the left knee, hip, shoulder, and arm all moving the club together. Your right knee should resist on the backswing as the right shoulder swings under your chin. This winding-up motion as the left shoulder moves slightly downward causes the arms and club to extend backward and then upward as the shoulder reaches a point directly under your chin. Your left shoulder should be well under your chin at the top of the backswing, with the shaft of the club approximately parallel to the ground and no weakening of the grip. When this position has been achieved you will feel

30

The backswing movement should be a "one-piece" action with the left knee, hip, shoulder, and arm all moving the club together. The right knee should resist on the backswing as the left shoulder swings under the chin.

At the top of the backswing, the left shoulder should be well under the chin, and the shaft of the club should be approximately parallel to the ground with no loss of control of the grip.

a tremendous resistance in your right side, and a stretched feeling in your left arm and left shoulder blade. The coiling action feels like the drawing back of a big rubber band, or the drawing back of an archer's bow as he prepares to shoot an arrow.

The club should be pushed away smoothly, working the hands and arms up into a position where you can start the downswing and create the acceleration that is vital to attain distance. When the club is at hip level, the clubface should be facing the ground. The shoulders should turn to their fullest extent, causing the entire weight of the body to coil behind the ball. Achieving the proper shoulder turn will enable the golfer—whatever his level of skill—to reach his personal distance potential. Without a proper shoulder turn, the responsibility for power lies in the hands instead of the legs and shoulders where it belongs.

The downswing for tee shots should be started with the lower half of the body, primarily the knees. The right knee, which has been resisting the coiling under of the left shoulder, should spring laterally toward the target, causing a counterclockwise turning of the hips. At the completion of the swing, the hips will actually face the target. Both knees should remain flexed, as they were at address, throughout the downswing.

At impact, the left hip should be out of the way and the left arm fully extended, with the weight predominantly on the left side.

The recoiling torso follows in behind the flow of force to a smooth, high finish. A high finish is a controlling factor of the swing.

The arms, hands, and clubhead follow the body and legs into the downswing. Your left side must clear out of the way before impact. Your left arm should be fully extended at impact. The control in the grip should be consistent in pressure throughout the swing. The left wrist through the hitting area and at contact should feel bent out or bowed toward the target, rather than in a cupped or broken position. The left wrist should actually face toward the ground at contact. Your right shoulder should swing down and under your chin.

33

This solid position of your left side pulling with great thrust through the ball will cause your entire right side (shoulder, hip, and knee) to swing down and under your chin. A characteristic of a sound swing is a high finish, with hands above the head and elbows above the shoulder. Many of the professionals on the tour don't finish this high all the time because they're trying to control the shot. The high finish applies mostly to the full swing.

When the swing is completed, the golfer should be facing the target, the left foot firmly planted and the right toe in contact with the ground.

When trying to hit a tee shot for both distance and accuracy, the full rhythmical motion of the swing must be maintained from the beginning to the finish. A high finish indicates that you've delivered the full thrust of your weight through the ball, leaving you fully uncoiled but still in a balanced position at the finish. If you swing *through* the ball, rather than *at* the ball, you will automatically produce a good follow-through. As you finish, your torso and right knee should be squarely facing the target with a nearly total weight shift to your left side and only enough weight remaining on your right toe to balance yourself.

How consistently you achieve this goal of hitting the ball straight and far down the fairway will depend solely on your personal ability to coordinate grip, stance, alignment, balance, and timing of the moving parts in the proper swing plane without losing control of the clubhead by your left side. Willingness to work with a teaching professional on a regular basis and sufficient time spent practicing will be vital.

If you try to think of all the fundamentals at one time, you will clutter your mind, creating "paralysis by analysis." Instead, practice one fundamental at a time and concentrate on each ingredient in sequence. If you are patient, eventually they will all fall into place and blend smoothly together.

fairway woods

by Mac Hunter, Sr.

The way the pros play the game today, there are not many occasions when they must use a wood off the fairway. Most can get sufficient distance out of their long irons to preclude the use of fairway woods for any but special shots or really long par 4s and 5s. With the 90-shooter, however, the story is different. For him, the fairway wood shot is an absolute necessity, for he can satisfy his need for distance only by the successful use of wood clubs.

It should be emphasized, though, that elements other than distance can at times be determining factors when club selection is made. For instance, if you are at 3-wood distance from a green but have a very poor lie, it might well be wise to consider a 5-wood or even an iron and settle for being a little short.

For some golfers the fairway woods are the toughest clubs to handle. This is so primarily because they don't trust the woods; they have too often failed to get the ball airborne. Fear of mis-hitting a shot makes a golfer apprehensive and tense. Then anything can happen, and usually does.

The proper way to hit a wood shot from the fairway is with confidence—confidence that is based on knowledge and understanding of the contemplated shot and an ability to pull it off. Generally speaking, the wood swing is more descending, coming into and through the ball, than most golfers would believe. If you try to lift or elevate the ball by raising your body in the hitting zone immediately before impact, you are making a bad mistake.

Any complete discussion of the fairway woods must, of course, include the brassie or 2-wood. This club is offered as an optional wood in a standard set of woods. Not many pros carry or find use for the 2-wood these days, and those who do select it only when the wind is strong enough to demand a low, quail-high shot. But whatever the situation, a superior lie is a requisite for the use of this club at all times. The positioning of the ball with the 2-wood is similar to that for the tee shot, except that the ball is played a shade farther back—off the extreme tip of the left heel. The purpose of this positioning of the ball is to ensure that it will be struck at almost the bottom of the swing arc and will be swept from the turf with only slight scarring of the ground.

The workhorse fairway wood for everyone, pro or weekend duffer, is the 3-wood. The 3-wood is lofted enough to get the ball up and winging when distance is needed and the lie is good. A 90 player could probably throw all his woods away except this club and play just as well or better than if he carried a full set. The swing to use with a 3-wood is almost the same as that which is used with the driver and 2-wood. It should be a full, free swing, not hurried or snatched. Because the shaft of the club is shorter than that of the driver, the swing arc is somewhat smaller and more easily controlled. The player may stand a bit closer to the ball when using this club. Otherwise the positioning is much the same as previously explained. If anything, the ball is struck a slightly more decisive blow, a characteristic that increases with each successive fairway wood as loft increases and club length shortens.

Specifically, the ball should be played slightly to the right of the left heel, but no more than a couple of inches to the right of the driving position. If all else goes right, this will enable the clubhead

The stance and swing used with the fairway woods is similar to that used with the driver except that the ball is played slightly to the right of the normal position used with the driver, and the ball is struck with a more decisive blow and with a slightly descending stroke.

to hit the ball slightly before the bottom of the swing arc is reached. Do not attempt to punch down on the ball. Keep the swing rhythmic and unhurried, not short and choppy.

A common mistake made by many golfers is to apply power when power is not necessary. If you'll remember to let the

clubhead do the work, you will reap a rich harvest from this simple cure-all.

Less delicate, perhaps, is the 4-wood. It is not often used by the majority of golfers, yet it is potentially the most useful of all the fairway woods for golfers shooting in the 90s. Its distance qualities

are good and it's easy to use. Its rather small head, thin face, and greater loft combine to force the ball to rise much faster than the 2-wood or 3-wood.

Another advantage of the 4-wood is its ability to get the ball up from rough or poor lies. Its knoblike head doesn't cut and

tangle in the grass like an iron club, but spreads it as it glides through. The wood can also be used successfully for hitting from a fairway bunker when the situation calls for distance.

When hitting a wood from sand be sure you have solid footing. Swing well within yourself and catch the ball clean, precisely at the base of your arc. Because of the 4-wood's shorter shaft, the player must stand closer to the ball and make sure that the sole is laid flat or flush to the ground at address. As with the 3-wood, the ball should be positioned a couple of inches inside the left heel for normal shots from normal lies. Employ the same swing that is used for all full wood shots. A concerted effort should be made to keep the head completely still and the eyes focused on the ball throughout the swing. The follow-through action should be low and extended. At the finish, the weight should be on the outside of the left foot and well toward the heel.

The 5-wood, like the 2-wood, is considered an auxiliary club, even though its popularity increases with every year as that of the 2-wood diminishes. The club can be useful in many situations that face the handicap golfer—fairway bunkers, for example, and in very deep rough and very poor lies. It's great when you want to get a ball up fast or sit it on the green softly. It can also be an asset for many golfers who have trouble with long irons—particularly the 2-iron and 3-iron.

Fairway woods are not difficult to use, but they do demand practice on a continual basis. More often than not, when managed correctly, they can reduce the score of a handicap golfer and will soon seem easier to use than the straight-faced irons. Don't be surprised if sets of woods as high as ten are someday offered as standard equipment. Lofted woods are more easily hit and controlled than long irons, and are ever increasing in popularity.

If one underlying thought were offered as a key to better fairway wood play it would be to swing the club head at all times, never forcing the shot but rather letting it happen.

by Zell Eaton

The major difference between wood and iron shots is that the latter must be struck with a descending blow. It's easy to remember: the nearer you get to the green, the more you must hit down on the ball.

There is no deep mystery to playing the irons efficiently. You must incorporate the same smooth timing that you use with the woods. The clubs get shorter and the stance changes, but otherwise the technique is much the same as with the woods.

THE LONG IRONS

Normally, you play the long irons from the same stance that you use for the drive—directly opposite the left heel. This somewhat forward position permits you not only to compensate for the longer irons but to get the ball up easier.

Obviously, the great problem most handicap golfers face when using the long irons is getting the ball to take flight. This results from a "feeling" that they cannot lift the ball with such a flat-faced club. It's a difficult feeling to lose. The effect is an inclination to lift up with the body in the act of hitting the ball—which produces a slice.

Again, you use the same swing that you use with the woods except that you stand a little bit closer to the ball as the shafts of the 1-iron, 2-iron, and 3-iron are shorter than the shafts of the woods.

At the same time, in playing the long irons, you must take a full backswing and make a full pivot just as in wood play. It is also very important that you stay down on the ball and reserve the use of the hands until the clubhead is in the hitting area, just as in hitting the woods.

There is little need to discuss the 1-iron, once called the driving iron. High handicappers should avoid this club like the plague. It's much too difficult to master for most golfers.

The 2-iron is something else. This is your heavy-artillery iron, used for distances up to 200 yards. Though it's advantageous for the average golfer to use a 5-wood rather than the 2-iron for such distance, the iron is best when playing into wind and keeping the ball low.

Grip firmly when using this club to keep the club from turning with the shock of heavy contact with the ball. The thin blade of the 2-iron or 3-iron offers little resistance if the ball is hit just slightly off center.

In taking your stance with the 2-iron or 3-iron, your feet should be square to the line of flight and not quite as wide as in hitting the woods. As in playing the woods, take the clubhead back low and slow with no cocking of the wrists until the hands have left the hip-line area on the backswing.

When using the 3-iron, play the ball back, perhaps an inch, from the position that you use with a 2-iron shot. Otherwise follow the same technique as with the 2-iron: firm grip, full swing, and cocking of the wrists at the hip-line area.

THE MEDIUM IRONS

The medium irons—4, 5, and 6—are not nearly as difficult to hit as the long irons. But putting the ball near your target is something else again. At any rate, most golfers who are consistently scoring in the 90s or 80s use these clubs with a lot more confidence. This is because the shorter clubs "feel" better and usually are played to their full distance.

The medium irons are double-duty clubs, however. For they are also valuable—depending upon your individual choice and feel—for stroke-saving chips.

Important to keep in mind when using these clubs is to hit the ball before taking a divot. If you take a divot behind the ball or where the ball is resting, you are wasting your power. The ball must be struck first and pinched against the turf before the clubhead goes "through" and takes the divot.

With the medium irons, the swing is naturally more upright, as you are standing closer to the ball. But the medium-iron swing is exactly the same mechanically as the long-iron swing. The fundamentals are the same. The left arm should be kept firmly straight and the right elbow should be kept close to the side. And the club should never be dropped below the horizontal at the top of the backswing.

As with all iron shots, these should be played with a firm grip and very strong wrists. On the backswing, they should be taken back low and slow, square against the target. The right wrist should hinge as the hands approach the level of the hips.

The stance for these clubs is relatively the same, with the feet square to the line of flight. But there is a slight difference with each iron as to the positioning of the ball. For the 4-iron shot, the ball should be played just ahead of the center line between the feet. The 5-iron stance has the ball on the center line between the feet. And with the 6-iron shot, the ball is positioned just slightly back of the center line.

Besides using the medium irons for full shots and chip shots, they are quite often used for the tee shot on par-3 holes. On these shots, they should be used exactly as on a fairway shot. No tee should be used. The reason for not using a tee is that, in hitting this type of shot, you want to "hold" on the green. To make your shot hold or bite, you must generate considerable backspin. This means that you must hit the ball first and then take a divot. It is difficult to do this if the ball has been teed.

The chip-and-run shot can be played with any club from the 4-iron to the 9-iron. But the handicap golfer can usually do better with this shot if he uses the 6-iron or 7-iron. The general rule is to use a club with just enough loft to take the ball to the green.

When playing this shot, the stance should be slightly open, with the arms straight and the weight on the left foot. The feet should be relatively close together and the ball played off the right foot so the ball is struck with a descending stroke.

It's important, too, to keep the face of the club square to the line at address and the hands slightly ahead of the ball. There should be but a minimum of wrist action as the club is taken back, and on the forward portion of the swing there should be no wrist action at all.

A complete discussion of the pitch and chip shots is included in chapter 7.

THE SHORT IRONS

The short irons—7, 8, 9—are the stroke savers of your set. These are the clubs which you should be able to hit with enough consistency to reach one-putt distance much of the time. Practice with them often, twice as much as with your driver.

Recall again that the short-iron swing is basically the same as for all other clubs except that on occasion you use a half-swing or three-quarters swing, depending upon distance. Because of the length of the clubs, the swing is more upright, of course, and the body turn is somewhat less as you move down with the clubs. Also, the stance gets narrower and is opened more as the clubs get shorter.

For best results play the ball near the center of the stance for all full shots, with about 60 percent of the weight on the left foot. And keep the hands ahead of the ball. High-handicap golfers start out this way at the address, but lose the position on the hit.

As with the other iron shots, the club should be taken back low and slow in a one-piece turning motion with the entire left side.

At the top of the backswing, much of the weight is on the right leg; the left knee is pointing in behind the ball; the hips have turned fully; the left shoulder has turned down and under the chin; and the left arm is fully extended to the eleven-o'clock position.

On the downswing, pull the club down and through the ball in a one-piece turning motion. Follow through strongly with the club pointing in the direction of the target.

the short game

7

by Jack Fleck

Year in and year out, a strong short game—or the lack of it—decides the fate of many players. And the longer one plays the game of golf, the more this is true. If you are past the age when the hips move freely, or have grown a slight paunch, you are bound to have trouble with your woods and long irons. But you can still save strokes in the "scoring zone"—from 70 yards out from the green.

Mastering the short game is just as important to the younger players and professional players. Good pitch and chip shots are the keys to getting into position for shorter putts—to save more pars and get more birdies.

Chipping is easier than pitching for the majority of players, since chips are normally shorter. But the shots are very similar in several respects, and the ability to master them depends upon practice, as with any shot.

Generally speaking, there are two types of chip shots and two types of pitch shots which all players should perfect: the chip-and-run and the soft chip, and the lofted pitch and low-running pitch.

49

Which one you should use in a particular situation is, of course, a good question. The best method of answering this question is to form a mental picture of the way you would like the ball to behave for the best results, and then use the club and stroke that will do the job.

There are several factors that you must take into consideration when choosing a club for a particular shot. You must check the contour of the green, the grain of the green, hazards between the ball and the green, and distance to the pin. If, for example, you are 30 yards from the pin, the green is relatively flat, and the grain of the green is *with* you, you may want to use a high-flying pitch, in order to produce backspin and stop the ball as quickly as possible. On the other hand, if the slope of the green is upward as you face it, and the grain of the green is against you, you will probably prefer a low-running pitch.

When pitching or chipping you use the same grip you use for all other clubs, but choke down on the club to ensure better control. The stance should be open (left foot withdrawn three or four inches from the line of flight) with the ball positioned off the left heel. It's also important for the knees to be slightly bent with a little more weight on the left foot than the right. Keep the hands forward of the shaft at address and keep them there when coming through the ball.

A chip shot is controlled with the left hand, so try to feel the back of the left hand swinging the club back, then leading down and going on through.

For a running chip shot from just off the green, I personally prefer to use the pitching wedge and to hit the ball just hard enough to land it on the green and run it to the hole. The shot must be played crisply. With a short backswing, keeping the club low to the ground, I cock my wrists very quickly; then, on the downswing, I uncock my wrists at precisely the moment I make contact with the ball. The follow-through is relatively short.

From just off the green, this is the way the chip shot is played by the majority of professionals. But many other players successfully employ the 8-iron or 9-iron for this particular shot. It doesn't matter which club you use, as long as you reach the green and run the ball up to the flag.

For a running chip shot from just off the green, assume a slightly
open stance with the heels about three inches apart and play the
ball so that the hands are well ahead of the clubhead. Also, be
sure that the majority of the weight of the body is on the left
side.

Use a relatively short backswing, keeping the club low to the ground, and cock the wrists as quickly as possible. Permit only a slight weight transfer to the right during the backswing.

On the downswing, uncock the wrists precisely at the moment the clubhead strikes the ball and use a relatively short follow-through. Don't look up until the ball is well on its way.

For longer chip shots, I use a longer backswing and cock the wrists a little more smoothly. Then I swing through the ball and follow through longer. Again, I prefer to use the pitching wedge, but a less-lofted club can also do the job.

Never move your head when chipping. It's important to anchor the head, as you do with all shots. Nor should you dip the body in an attempt to "help" the shot—to give it some lift with a scooping action. Let the club do the work.

When the green is very soft, and you want to chip closer to the flag, use a high, soft chip. For this shot, you should use the pitching wedge or 9-iron. Play the shot from a slightly open stance, the ball just forward of the centerline. Then choke down on the club and play the ball back toward the right foot. Once again, you should cock the wrists quickly so that the hands will be moving ahead of the club. Make sure you hit down and through.

As you move back to a distance of about 20 to 30 yards from the green, you are moving out of chipping range and dealing exclusively with pitching shots. If the terrain is flat and firm and the green is wide open, you can either stay with the less-lofted irons for a low-flying pitch that will give you a good run, or use a wedge and hit to a spot on the green closer to the pin. In either case, the ball is played like a chip shot except that the arc of the swing must be longer to get more distance.

For a high, soft pitch, which is normally used to clear a hazard, you should use a 9-iron or wedge and play the shot in a normal manner, considering the distance.

An additional approach shot which can come in handy is the punch shot. To achieve a well-hit punch shot you must make some adjustments in your stance, however. Almost all of your weight should be on your left foot. In fact, you should actually lean in the direction of the shot. Your hands should be well ahead of the ball, which is played off the right foot. Then, keeping your left arm and wrists firm as the club meets the ball, you should follow through low, with your club pointing in the direction of the target.

The punch shot is usually used when fighting a crosswind or a wind that's blowing in your face. The intention is to keep the ball low so that the effect of the wind will be kept to a minimum.

The stance for the pitching clubs gets narrower and more open as the shorter sticks are used. Normally a pitching wedge or 9-iron is used. The ball should be played in a normal position.

Little pivot should be used when pitching to the green, and it is not necessary to take a long swing. Length of the swing depends upon distance to the green. The longer the distance, the longer the swing.

A *relatively high follow-through is required, and the player should be facing the target with the weight almost entirely on the left foot at the finish of the swing.*

One final thought: chip and pitch shots are finesse shots, not muscle shots. Choke down on the club and try for control rather than distance. You have a wide assortment of clubs to use. There is never any need to force a shot or go all out.

trouble
shots

by Jimmy Powell

Everyone gets into trouble at one time or another. And it's a safe bet that most golfers who are attempting to break 90 get in trouble often enough to cost them strokes in almost every round. It is essential, therefore, to learn to handle "trouble shots"—the most common, at least—so that you will be prepared when trouble strikes.

Trouble shots are not difficult, but all trouble shots demand application of fundamentals and a great deal of practice.

PLAYING FROM TALL GRASS

The most common trouble is heavy rough. Heavy rough, in this case, is defined as long grass.

The difficulty of hitting from long grass was plainly evident during the 1972 Tournament of Champions at La Costa Country Club in California when the rough was largely responsible for keeping all but seven golfers from bettering par for the four-day event.

59

When playing a shot from high grass, study the amount and length of the grass. If the grass is thin and not too high, hit the ball with the clubface open and aim to the left. If the grass is high and thick, use an upright swing and hit the ball with a descending stroke.

Playing from high grass requires several types of special shots. But the common denominator for all rough play is to get the ball up and flying very quickly. For this reason, it is extremely foolish for a golfer to select a wood for anything other than a perfect lie in the rough. It is almost impossible to hit a good shot with a wood from the rough.

It is also very difficult to hit a good shot from long grass with a long iron. Unless the club can hit the ball with no grass in between, use a more lofted iron and sacrifice distance.

The basic way to play these shots is to play the ball back toward the right foot and hit with a descending stroke just as you would for all shots with the medium and short irons. And try to be compact and firm with the shot right through to the end.

UPHILL, DOWNHILL, AND SIDEHILL LIES

With an uphill lie, the ball will go higher and not quite as far as it would if the ball were on a flat lie. You should therefore compensate for this by using one club more than you normally would. In other words, if the shot would normally call for a 5-iron, use a 4-iron.

When playing this shot, open your stance and take the club straight back from the ball and hit down and through as you would for most shots. But keep the club and the hands in a normal position—unless you want to keep the ball down. To keep the ball down, move the hands slightly forward. To keep the ball up, move the hands slightly back.

With a downhill lie, the center of gravity will be forward. So to offset this unbalance, bend the uphill knee so that the hips are level and play the ball a little to the right of center with an open stance. Generally, it's a good plan to use one club shorter, too, when playing this shot, since you will contact the ball sooner, and it's often difficult to get the ball up.

Use a normal takeaway action, but on the downswing follow the contour of the ground and hit down on the ball without raising the body at impact.

When playing an uphill lie, the ball should be played forward in the stance and the clubhead should be swung so that it follows the slant of the ground. As much weight as possible should be placed on the left foot at address so that the weight does not slide too much to the right on the backswing and stay too much to the right when the ball is hit.

62

With a downhill lie, play the ball slightly toward the right foot if the lie is extreme. If the lie is less severe, play it more toward the left foot. Try to refrain from letting the weight get too much on the left foot.

With a sidehill lie and the ball below your feet, it is best to use one club longer to compensate for the distance you are above the ball. It also can be helpful to aim slightly left, because the ball has a tendency to travel to the right from this lie.

64

If the ball is resting on a sidehill lie—and lower than your feet—use one club longer and aim slightly left of the target, for the ball will have a tendency to go to the right. And play the ball in the center of a square stance. However, the stance should be slightly wider than normal to help in maintaining your balance. Bend the knees more than usual and keep the weight back on the heels.

If the ball is resting on a sidehill lie and above your feet, use the same club you would normally use for the shot, but flex your knees slightly and keep your weight on the balls of your feet. The ball, being higher, will be closer to you, of course, so shorten your grip on the club so that the clubhead rests on the ground without the arms being bent any more than for a normal shot. Since the ball will have a tendency to go to the left of the target, aim slightly to the right.

WHEN TREES ARE THE PROBLEM

When you are confronted with trees on the course, you have three choices: over, under, or around. To go over a tree, you must use a lofted club, one that will get the ball high enough to clear the obstacle. There's little to add to this except that when it's necessary to get the ball up quicker than usual you can "help" the shot by keeping the hands slightly behind the ball at address and let the club work through and under the ball by using a bit of wrist action.

To go under a tree, you must use a less lofted club, like the 2-iron or 3-iron. It's wise also to choke up on the club according to the distance you need. Seldom should you grip it full length. Play the ball slightly back of the normal position and keep the hands slightly ahead of the ball at address.

Punch the ball rather than hit it. To do this use no more than a three-quarter swing, keeping the right elbow close to the side. Keep the left arm and both wrists stiff throughout the swing, and use no pivot whatsoever. Finally, for a minimum of loft and a maximum of accuracy, keep the follow-through low and directed toward the target.

Going around a tree is usually a more complicated operation. In most cases it requires either an intentional hook or an intentional slice. Both of these more sophisticated shots are detailed in chapter 16.

When it is necessary to hit under a low-hanging tree, a less lofted club should be used and the ball played back in the stance to ensure that the ball will stay low.

When hitting from bare ground, it is imperative for the head and body to remain steady throughout the swing. Whether a wood or iron is used, the ball must be struck with a slightly descending stroke so that the ball is contacted before the ground. If the club hits the ground before hitting the ball, it will bounce and the shot will be topped.

WHEN HITTING OFF BARE GROUND

The greatest difficulty in hitting off a bare lie is to get the ball flying, especially with a wood or a long iron. The only answer to this is to be extremely careful to hit the ball before hitting the ground.

When close to the green, the problem is not so bad. Use a pitching wedge and address the ball off the right foot, with the hands slightly ahead of the clubhead and with most of the weight on the right foot. Then hit down on the shot, making sure you contact the ball first and then the ground. Allow for roll. You should get a low shot and 50 percent roll.

WHEN THE BALL IS IN WATER

The best advice available for playing a ball out of water is—don't. It's extremely chancy to attempt an important shot from a lie in water, even if part of the ball is showing above the water.

Arnold Palmer's attempt to hit from a lie of this type in the 1972 Greater Greensboro Open should be evidence that the shot is a risk even for the most talented professionals. He lost the tournament as a result of this shot.

If you must take the gamble, there are important rules to follow. First, you must play the ball like a ball buried in sand. You should use an explosion shot. This is best done with a 9-iron or pitching wedge. A cut shot should be played. Only with a cut shot, which allows the blade of the club to slice through the water, can you hope to succeed.

The cut shot is played, of course, by opening the blade of the club and opening the stance, which causes the clubhead to move into the ball from outside the intended line of flight, cutting under the ball and imparting clockwise, or slice, spin on the ball. It's a delicate shot, too tough for most 90s shooters.

sand
play

by Dale Andreason

If you want to hit a good sand shot, you need the proper club—the sand wedge. As a rule of thumb, it is best for a woman player to use a club with no more than a D-2 swing weight and for a man to use a club with no more than an E swing weight. The sand wedge should be heavier than a normal 9-iron, but still easy to control. With a little experimenting you can find a sand wedge that fits you.

Before setting yourself up to swing, check the texture of the sand very closely. Check to see if it is wet, hard, loose, or powdery. In heavy, wet sand, which is more compact, the ball will tend to come up more quickly. Loose and powdery sand has the reverse effect. The texture of the sand is extremely important because you are supposed to hit the sand, not the ball. And because you hit the sand and not the ball, there is more room for error than with any other shot. Still, there's no need to fear bunker shots if you first learn the basic fundamentals and practice them often.

For a normal sand shot from a flat lie, your stance should be open, with the hands ahead of the clubhead and 60 percent of the weight on the left side.

The length of the backswing is limited by the length of the shot to be made. There should be practically no weight shift to the right during the backswing.

In setting yourself up for a sand shot, you must first establish a firm footing by twisting your feet down into the sand. This will also permit you to note the depth of the sand and its texture. Concentrate on looking at the sand where you want to contact it. And remember that it is against the rules to touch your club to the sand as you address the ball. The sand shot requires feel and imagination. Oddly enough, it takes more gentleness than power.

Don't try to hit too hard. Think of the sand shot as being more like a 20-to-30-yard pitch or approach shot—but strike slightly behind, under, and through the ball, not down. It's a sweeping action, not a digging action. Relate the length of your backswing and the amount of sand you want to take to the length of the shot. If it's a short shot, make a slightly more abrupt arc and contact the sand farther behind the ball. If it's a long shot, take a wider arc and contact the sand closer to the ball. Hit the sand from one-half to two inches behind the ball, depending on the length of the shot, texture of the sand, and type of lie.

You may be faced with a surface lie, where the ball is lying on top of the sand; a "fried-egg" lie, where the ball has landed in the bunker and is partially buried with a crater effect around the ball; or a buried lie, where the ball is just partially visible in the sand. Moreover, the lie may be uphill, downhill, or level.

When playing from a surface lie, you should choke the club down about three inches, and 60 percent of your weight should be on the left foot, where it will stay during the backswing. If your weight shifts to the right foot there is a good chance you will overswing, lose control of the club, or slip in the sand.

Play the ball off the left heel, and pull the left foot back a few inches to provide an open stance. This will permit you to cut slightly across the sand without the left leg being in the way. The clubface should be held open about 45 degrees, which will allow the club to work into the sand and under the ball.

The backswing should be started very smoothly by taking the club back straight with the left hand. This gives you solid left side control and keeps the backswing short and compact.

Important to remember is that the head should be kept steady and behind the ball and that the left hand keep the toe of the

The clubface should be slightly open at impact with the sand.
This will permit the club to work into the sand and under the
ball. A "straight" clubface has a tendency to turn.

club open after the club has gone through the ball. This action causes the ball to come out high and light with a great deal of backspin.

When playing from a fried-egg lie, you use basically the same technique, though the wrists break a little more and the downswing is a sharper, crisper stroke. You should get a feeling of bumping or exploding the sand with this shot. The clubface should enter the sand a little more square, perhaps, and near the crest of the crater around the ball.

With a buried lie, you should play the ball a little more toward the center of your feet. Your stance, weight, and position should be the same as that used with the fried-egg lie, but the clubface should be closed a bit, as the sand will tend to open it at impact. The swing should be rhythmic, with a little wrist break, then down and through the sand. The downward movement of the clubface will make the ball pop up in the air. Distance of the shot determines the amount of sand you should take and how much to accelerate the clubhead.

A buried uphill lie requires a different technique. The stance should be very open and the feet should be aimed about 45 degrees to the left. Although the feet are aiming way to the left, it is easy to turn the hips back squarely to the intended line. This helps to maintain balance. The clubface should be square and the weight must be maintained on the left side or left foot. Because of the up-slope, the club should be held slightly above the sand and about one inch behind the ball. The left hand takes the club straight back in a low sweeping motion with a minimum of wrist break. The follow-through is upward while maintaining the weight on the left foot.

The buried downhill lie is the most feared of sand shots. But it is not a difficult shot if the basic fundamentals are followed. With this shot, you should choke down on the club and keep the weight on the left foot. If the downslope is very severe, you should try to dig in more with the right foot and try not to let more than 70 percent of your weight be on the left foot. The ball should be played near the center of the stance. Usually the clubhead should be slightly open, but if the slope is very severe, it should be square or closed.

On the backswing, try to take the club straight back while being careful to keep it from hitting the sand. On the downswing, the

When playing a ball on the upslope of a trap, use a very open stance and hold the club farther down the shaft. Keep the weight on the left foot.

When playing a ball on a downslope, keep only about 70 percent of the weight on the left side, and play the ball slightly back of the center of the stance.

left hand should bring the clubhead into the sand about two inches or so behind the ball, and the toe of the clubhead should be open or as square as possible. This will permit the clubhead to work under the ball and give it the backspin required to get the ball near to the hole.

One additional shot worth mentioning is the punch shot from the sand. This is a shot that is often used with 100 yards to go to the target. For this shot, you should dig your feet well into the sand and, again, keep 60 percent of the weight on the left foot. The ball should be played near the center of the stance. Either a sand wedge or a 9-iron can be used for this shot, but you should concentrate on taking the club back straight with both hands, keeping the left heel down and the weight on the left foot. On the downswing, concentrate on swinging the club down to the ball, hitting the ball first and then the sand. It is important to keep the head still.

In summary, then: (1) use the proper club, (2) position your stance solidly by twisting your feet in the sand, (3) determine which technique to use for the shot, (4) look at the sand and not the ball, and (5) sweep the club back and through the ball.

putting

by Ellsworth Vines

Unlike most other aspects of golf, putting is one area in which for the most part a player can make his own rules and work out the mechanics of stroking the ball to suit himself. No particular grip, stance, or stroke has been proved superior to all others. You can use any grip as long as it's comfortable, any stance that is legal, and any stroke that will move the ball on a straight line to the cup.

Yet there are guidelines that are usually helpful to the beginning player or the player who is having a problem with putting. Most, of course, concern the stroke. How you grip the putter is entirely up to you. You can hold it like a broom if that gets results. Most professionals, however, use the reverse overlapping grip, with the left forefinger riding on top of the right pinkie. And some even use the ten-finger grip, or baseball grip as it's often called. And many just use the standard overlapping grip.

You can stand as you wish as long as you avoid straddling the ball. You should know, however, that the majority of good golfers

The grip used for putting should be determined by personal preference. Most popular type used by the touring professionals is the reverse-overlap, which has the left forefinger overlapping the fingers of the right hand and the thumbs straight down the shaft.

A good stance for either a long or a short putt has the weight equally distributed on both feet and the body bent over just enough so that the eyes are directly over the ball when looking down on the ball. The knees should be bent slightly.

The most vital element for successful putting is to be sure to line up the face of your putter perfectly square to the intended path of the ball.

use a square stance, with the toes of both feet parallel to the line of the intended putt. Such a stance lends itself to the most accurate use of the arms, hands, and eyes.

Here are a few more fundamentals you should think about no matter what personal style you may develop.

The putt is essentially a hand and arm shot, played largely without movement of the body. The wrists are the hinges and the club is swung like a pendulum. The putter is brought back straight from the ball and returned to the ball along the same line. This is important. There's no way to putt effectively unless you stroke with the face of the club square to the hole. If, during your stroke, you open or close the face of the club you will be off line. The length of your backswing will depend on the distance you are from the hole. The longer the putt, the longer the backswing.

The putt should be struck with the right hand. The putt really is the only shot in golf that is actually *struck* in the sense that there is actually a positive act of striking the ball.

The duty of the left hand is to serve as control, leading the stroke through and toward the hole, while the right hand commands.

An additional element in the putting stroke is the matter of spin—specifically, overspin. The purpose in putting is to move the ball in the direction of the hole and to keep the ball moving until it arrives. Stroking the ball with an upward motion, which produces overspin, helps it roll better and reach the objective. There's nothing so distressing as seeing a ball die a few inches from the hole or at the lip of the hole. Overspin reduces the chances of this happening. Keeping the putter low to the ground throughout the stroke will produce proper roll and spin.

Another fundamental that all players should heed is to keep the head down and not follow the track of the ball to the hole. It's often disaster to look up. When a player looks up, he pulls his body and arms off line, and therefore the putt. It's a good plan to try to see only the putter head strike the ball.

To putt well, one must develop a feel for distance and direction, especially distance. Most three-putt greens are the direct result of a player's inability to judge the distance from the ball to the

With all putting strokes, the clubhead should be taken back squarely from the ball and kept very close to the ground. This will put overspin on the ball, which will encourage a truer roll.

For a short putt, there is very little movement of the body,
whether the wrist-putting method is used or the arm-and-
shoulder method. The clubhead should be taken straight back
from the ball, slowly and smoothly, and returned somewhat
faster. The ball should be struck sharply.

The follow-through for a short putt should be roughly equal in distance to the distance the club was taken back. Throughout the stroke, the head should remain in place.

For a long putt, the club should be taken back a greater distance and a greater wrist break used. Note here that the wristbreak in the right hand controls the backstroke.

The follow-through for a long putt should be roughly equal in distance to the distance the club was taken back. The clubhead should still be square with the line to the target.

hole. On the other hand, seldom does a putt stray off the line enough to get you in trouble.

Learning to judge distance is not something a player can be taught, at least via words. Learning to judge distance can only be accomplished through practice and more practice. Many high-handicap players find it helpful to imagine a circle three feet in diameter surrounding the hole, then to putt for the circle. Enlarging the regulation hole to a proportion that the mind can more easily accept can be an aid to a weekend player.

So practice for distance. If your distance is correct, you'll eliminate those three-putt greens and knock off a lot of strokes. All players who shoot over 90 have too many three-putt greens. Eliminate these, and you're sure to be gnawing on the door of the 80s.

The grain and condition of the green are important factors too. Against the grain, you must strike the ball harder, and with the grain you must strike it more softly. Determining the grain—which way the grass grows—is usually very easy: if the grass is shiny the grain is with you; if it's somewhat darker it's running against you.

Uphill slopes and downhill slopes can affect the roll too. But if the grain and the slope run in opposite directions they may cancel each other out.

On the matter of direction, there is little to be said. You either have a sense of judging the direction of a particular putt or you don't have. Like distance, in a sense, it cannot be taught or learned from a book. Helpful, however, is to imagine a path from the ball to the hole—about a foot wide on longer putts and four inches wide on shorter putts—and to attempt to steer the ball within that path, instead of on a "line." Practice will develop this sense if you work at it.

What's the best practice procedure? Begin by practicing the short putts first. Start with two-foot putts and putt for several minutes or until you hit several without missing. Then putt from four feet, five feet, and so on, up to ten feet. And practice where the surface is relatively smooth. This will permit you to learn to judge distance while you're also learning to stroke the ball in the proper manner and to find the right line. The breaking putts should be practiced only after hitting straight putts from varying distances with success.

How long should you practice? No longer than thirty minutes each session. Once you lose concentration it's useless to continue. But practice often and before each round. You're throwing away strokes if you eliminate a session on the practice green before starting a round.

Seldom does a professional golfer start a round of golf without practicing his putting. And usually he won't stop practicing until he's making the putts, until he has the "feel." Once he gets this feel, however, he stops. To overpractice could use it up.

Remember that putting is half the game. On a regulation course, you can expect to take at least 36 strokes on the putting greens. This makes a two-foot putt just as important as a good drive. Don't slight your putting.

the
repeating
swing

11

by Mike Smith

When golf writers of another era referred to Ben Hogan as "The Mechanical Man," they showed no lack of respect. Nor do today's writers when they describe Gene Littler as "Gene the Machine." The writers are indeed complimenting these fine players for having achieved what all intelligent and energetic golfers try to achieve—a repeating swing.

Consistency—the ability to repeat the same physical movements with rhythm, timing, coordination—is the objective of most of the effort put in by the talented golfer on the practice tee. And it's a prime essential for the golfer trying to break into the 80s. For lack of consistency is the main thing that separates the low-handicap golfer from the duffer who hits a fine shot only to follow it with a bewildering mis-hit.

Evidence of the consistent swing—the repeating swing—is fascinatingly apparent in a study of almost any golf photographer's photo files. As insurance against failure to end up with a desired photo, most photographers use precautionary procedures. They take the same picture with three different lens openings, or from three different angles. The golf photographer has a peculiar problem. Live action on the course gives him only one chance at a picture. On the practice tee, he is not so concerned with the proper exposure as he is with snapping the action at a precise point in the swing. He will frequently take two or more shots of a player hitting the same type of shot, hoping to portray the hands at impact, or the player's foot position at the start of the downswing, or the position of the legs at impact.

Since the entire swing takes place in about a second and a half, the lensman doesn't have much room for error. He, too, must develop a keen sense of timing and coordination. He must develop a repeating shutter press.

Consequently, a look into a golf photographer's photo files will show not only the ability of the photographer to repeat in flicking the camera shutter but the sheer consistency in the swings of the better players.

Think about how often you hear a golfer remark: "Last week I was hitting the ball real good, but this week I'm all over the place."

And then, you'll hear: "I can't figure it out. I was hitting it real good during the first round, but today I couldn't hit a barn."

Naturally, the problems could be emotional, but a greater probability is that the various golfers with obvious problems never developed a consistent swing. While the par-breaking player has the consistency that comes from a repeating swing, the less than expert player lacks it and doesn't take the steps to acquire it.

The principles of repetitiveness in a physical movement toward achieving a given objective are simple enough to grasp. Whether it's pitching pennies, throwing darts, or hitting a ball, the movements required must be isolated, then put together in a simple pattern, and then the pattern must be made as mechanical as possible.

Physical movements can be made mechanical—automatic —by practice. Practice is a key factor. But practice alone isn't the answer. Many a handicap golfer has indeed developed a remarkable consistency—for doing the wrong thing. He may have a well-grooved, repeating swing. But, unfortunately, his repeating swing slices the ball

91

every time or hooks it every time. And the more he practices, the more he ingrains his swing faults into muscle memory.

So an imperative prerequisite to intelligent practice is to understand the movements that will result in the ball being hit straight and at a tolerable trajectory. Then all movements that don't help achieve the objectives can be dropped. From that point on, practice will make for constructive repetitiveness.

Basically, then, what we are saying is that the formula for a repeating swing, the formula that all first class players use, is:

(1) application of sound fundamentals as pertain to the grip, stance, backswing, and downswing;

(2) the putting together of these ingredients in a simple pattern while discarding unnecessary and noncontributing motions;

(3) continued practice until the movements become wholly automatic.

practice

by Bill Ogden

Nobody ever became good at golf (or anything else) without practicing a lot. And nobody ever remained good at the game without continuing to practice. It's unfortunate, therefore, that many golfers don't have sufficient time or desire to practice. But unfortunate, too, is the fact that most golfers who do practice, practice poorly, practice without meaning, and just waste their time. Intelligent practice is the key to improvement.

Intelligent practice doesn't mean just banging out a bucket of balls on the driving range with a driver and 3-wood. We have all seen golfers who show up at the practice range with a couple of clubs and proceed to hit balls in wild abandon, as hard as they can, from the high rubber tee on the rubber mat. And some of these golfers are reasonably proficient—at driving the ball from the tee and the mat. But how many times during a round of golf do you hit from a tee? And how many times do you get a good lie for your fairway shot, discounting the fact that the mat is not turf and doesn't act like turf? If you're going to improve, you've got to spend time on the stroke-saving shots, on the shots you most use, on the shots that are obviously causing you trouble.

Few golfers practice from the rough, for example. Yet the shot from the rough will face most golfers who are shooting in the 90s time and again. And few golfers practice hitting from a bunker, though this is a difficult shot for most golfers. And these shots are just two of a myriad of trouble shots many golfers neglect when they're visiting the range. How many golfers work on the mechanics of hitting a ball from a downhill lie or an uphill lie or a sidehill lie? Or from under a tree? Few, to be sure. But these are the shots that a golfer will face when he's on the course. And these are the shots that a golfer must practice.

"Fine," you say, "but where do I start and what do I do?" Logically, you start by working on your swing and loosening your muscles. And logically you start with the shorter clubs and work your way up to the longer clubs. It only makes sense. A boxer warms up, and so does a runner and so does a baseball pitcher. A golfer should too.

Start with the 9-iron—or perhaps the wedge—and hit a dozen balls, then move up a club. But don't move up just because you've hit twelve balls. Work with the club until you're sure you've progressed, worked out the wrinkles. Then continue on up to the low-numbered clubs and on to the woods. But spend more time with the high-numbered clubs than all of the others. These are the clubs that will lower your score quickest—at least if you're shooting in the 90s.

Don't hurry your shots. Rest between shots. Consider what you did; consider the results. If you sliced the ball, try to figure out why, or see a professional. Or return to the basics: check your grip and stance, position at the top, etc.

Don't just swing. Swing with a purpose. Hit toward a target. Pick out a marker or a spot on the edge of the driving range and hit toward that. This is the place to cultivate your swing and to gain control.

Practice from a bunker if a bunker is available. Hit woods from thin lies and irons from the rough. And avoid the rubber mats and the practice tee as much as you can. The tees are too high for the majority of golfers, and the mats too unlike the turf on a course.

You can hit six inches to the rear of a ball when it's on a mat and get a good shot. On the grass, you cannot; you'll get a "fat" shot.

You should also spend time just learning the distance you can get with each club. This is important. It does you no good to pinpoint the distance from your ball to the flag if you're not very sure which club you should use for that particular distance. Average distances for a club, often printed in books, are sometimes misleading to the handicap golfer and cause him much trouble. Make it a point to know your own distances with the clubs in your bag.

And don't forget putting when you go to a range. It's fully as important to practice with your putter as it is with other clubs. Putting, after all, is half the game. And set goals when you practice. Think as you would on a course, but don't worry too much about holing each putt. Concentrate more on rolling the ball well.

Instead of just dropping a dozen balls on one spot and hitting them alike, put them in a circle. This will make sure that each putt is different—of a different length.

Another good way to practice on the range is to "play" your home course or the course you play most and then play each hole—shot by shot—exactly as you would if present on the course. Let's say, for example, the first hole is par-4, 400 yards long. So take out your driver and hit down the middle at a marker sign. Did it go 200 yards? Then you have a wood shot or a long iron shot of 200 more yards. So pick out a club and shoot for the "green," making sure that you aim at a yardage marker to check the result. If you came up short or were off to the side, estimate the yardage for your following shot, then change clubs and try it. If you came up short by 25 yards, take out your wedge or your chipping club and try to hit a spot about 25 yards away. How close did you come? Fifteen feet? Give yourself a five. You obviously can't putt on a practice range, so count two putts if within 20 feet and three if farther out.

Now, play the next hole, and so on down the line. It's an entertaining way to practice and gives you a chance to use all the clubs and to work on control and judgment of distance.

Don't forget hazards. If a hole has a hazard along the left of the fairway, aim to the right when you drive on that hole. If you miss the fairway, play it that way. Play as you would on the real course.

Another suggestion for interesting practice is to imagine a hole that you often play which requires, perhaps, a drive and a short iron. Then change your clubs: instead of a driver, use a 3-wood off the tee and approach with a mid-iron. This method of practice can sharpen your skills with various clubs and give more variety to your practice session.

Consider, too, that practice at home can improve your skills, especially at putting. You can putt on a carpet or hit into a net or just swing the club. It's true that with a net you don't know where your shots are going—if they're hooking or slicing. But you gain rhythm and timing and develop the muscles involved in the swing.

Practice pays off—whatever your method. So visit a range as often as you can and supplement this practice with practice at home. And when the weekend arrives and you walk on the course, you will feel better and do better.

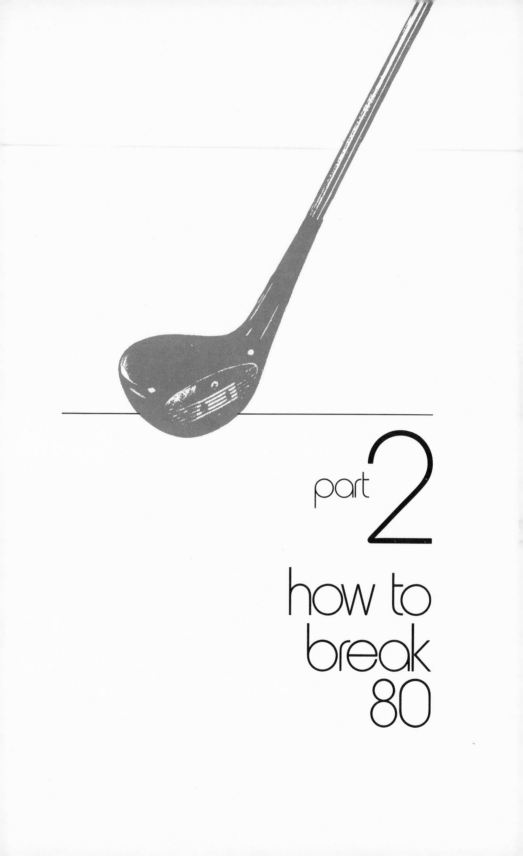

part 2

how to
break
80

into the
sweet
70s

Anyone who can break 80 with regularity belongs to an elite group. For breaking 80 is no snap for anyone. It's a goal worth striving for, and I promise that the first time you crack into the 70s, you'll stride off the course with the elation of a man who's just scored a hole-in-one. And in many ways, the feat will be more difficult, for it takes not just one luck shot, but a series of well-planned strokes on eighteen consecutive holes.

To break 80 you must plan your game hole by hole and shot by shot, using your knowledge of the course and judgment of playing conditions, and you have to have a sound game and a complete one. You still don't have to be very young or strong, or very long off the tee. However, the six-to-eight-handicapper must have a reliable short game that will often save his pars when he misses greens in regulation figures. A computer survey of play on the Professional Golfers Association tour revealed that the average touring pro hit only 12 of 18 greens in a round. Yet these same golfers all equaled or bettered par in their average rounds. This simply means that their approaching, pitching, chipping, and putting were good enough to rescue their pars after they had mis-hit their second shots.

A good all-round short game includes the ability to control the ball after it lands—especially on iron shots. The low-handicapper soon learns that putting backspin on the ball does not require a special stroke or a cut shot of any sort. He knows that every shot lofted into the air has backspin on it—otherwise it couldn't rise as it does. So he gets ball control by selection of the right iron and positioning the ball properly at address. The loft of the clubface and the weight distribution in the sole of the club do the rest.

However, a certain amount of finesse is required for various types of pitches around the green. A carefully gauged pitch-and-run shot is a must in the repertoire, as is the soft lob shot, and the low-flying wedge shot with extra backspin. These stroke-saving shots can save a par when a disastrous bogey or double bogey seems certain. They can be self-taught in practice and require no esoteric knowledge or instruction, assuming all your swing fundamentals are under control. For example, if you want to hit the wedge high and soft, as an experienced player you'll intuitively tilt the face back a little to give it more loft; and you'll make the stroke slowly and gently.

The low handicapper must know how to get out of trouble *and get close*. In other words it's not enough to simply escape, which is all you need in order to break 90. You have to escape almost infallibly, and do it well enough to save your par. This means practicing awkward shots from sand traps, from the rough and hard ground, in fact from all sorts of bad lies. Once you know you can extricate yourself from these tough predicaments without sacrificing more than one stroke, you'll never panic.

Playing in the 70s takes a lot more than just paddling the ball somewhere down the fairway and hoping Lady Luck is with you. You have to pick your spots at all times—off the tee, and to the green. If your view from the tee of a par-4 tells you the pin is cut to the right portion of the green, you'll try to place your tee shot on the left side of the fairway. This will give you more green to work with on your second shot, allowing you a larger target area.

As you size up your approach shot, you may note that the green is steeply banked with the lowest slope in front. This means that any medium or short iron with appreciable bite will spin back toward the front part of the green. So your careful observation can pay off. You either run the ball up to the hole, or aim to the top part of the flag and allow for the ball to draw back to the hole after it lands.

These, of course, are examples of knowledge and playing strategy. You need them—but without one other important factor all your efforts can lead to frustration in the scoring department. That factor is *putting*. There are very few low-handicap golfers who are not excellent putters. The old saying "Drive for show and putt for dough" still holds. It's the golfer who dunks those crucial five-footers who walks off with the Class "A" Championship or the big Calcutta pool at your club.

Consistently good putting can put you in a class by yourself. You don't need a golf course to practice your stroke. A putter in your office, living room, or hotel room will keep your hands sensitive to the putting stroke. When on the tour, Ben Hogan sank more ten-footers into the bottom of the bedpost than any other traveling man alive. So, practice those putts every chance you get. It could get you into the high 70s faster than any other improvement in your game.

course
knowledge

by Deane Beman

It has often been said that to do his best a golfer must play the course and not his opponent. The statement is sound. A golfer who wants to improve must acquaint himself intimately with the course he is playing or is about to play.

Most championship courses have a number of hazards—and aids too—that are hidden from sight. A golfer should know these "blind" hazards and aids and use them to advantage. Unseen bunkers, water hazards, slopes, and rough are "obvious" ones.

You should also know the distance to the greens from areas of the fairways and the size of the greens before you play a course, other than in practice.

Often overlooked by a great many golfers are slopes on the fairway and condition of the turf in various areas. Too many golfers grab a driver on every tee even if it means landing on a slope or in an unknown area.

There's no great advantage to going all out—hitting for distance—if your second shot must be made off a slope or uneven ground. Far better to know that the slope or questionable terrain is out there waiting for dummies and to play the ball short to more favorable ground.

Generally speaking, there are fourteen holes on an average course which seemingly call for use of the driver. But for knowledgeable golfers, only eight or nine might call for a driver. Which eight or nine depends upon your knowledge of the course and where potential problems lie.

To repeat: this knowledge results from knowing where the problems are located and the distance to these dangers. It's imperative that a serious golfer step off the distance to the various hazards and *know* the course he's playing.

A common practice of the majority of professionals playing on tour is to pick out an object (a tree, sprinkler head, or perhaps a bush) adjacent to the spot where their ball has landed, note the object on their scorecard, then pace off the distance from the object to the green. This gives them accurate knowledge about distance and club selection for later rounds.

Similarly, my method is to hit from the tee and if the drive is average to note the position in relation to a tree or other object lateral to the ball, then to hit to the green and pace off the distance to the center of the green. If the shot is accurate, I note this too and the club that was used. If the shot was long or short, I note this fact. Then I know the distance to the green from a certain point and the club to be used for the particular distance.

Later, of course, the selection can be changed according to the wind or other factors. If the wind is against me in a later round, to cite an example, I can add one club; if the wind is behind me I can drop one club.

Knowledge about the size of the various greens is important too. You should know if a green is a "one-club" green or a "two-club" green. That is, you should know if a green can be reached with one of two clubs or only one club. A green that is deep is usually the former while a smallish green is a one-club green. This knowledge can serve you at a later date when the pin is in front or to the rear of the green or when the wind is a factor.

One caution here: don't count on getting your yardages from others—even a caddy. Though they could be correct, it's quite possible that they'll be incorrect. If you take your own yardages, you'll *know* they are accurate.

There's no place for guesswork when you're playing golf in a serious manner or for a living. And it stands to reason that a golfer knowledgeable about course conditions, distances, and the like will have an advantage over golfers who are guessing and hoping for the best.

strategy off the tee

by *Jim Jamieson*

Once you have developed your game to the point that you can score fairly well, you will become aware that most of your problems result from poor drives. Put another way, many of your problems can be directly attributed to lack of ability to position the ball in a desirable area, careless play, or faulty strategy.

Lack of ability, of course, can be corrected only by practice—correct practice and long practice. But careless play and faulty strategy can easily be amended to improve your game. All you need do is to learn to think and abide by some "rules" that professionals use and use to advantage.

It has often been said that the putting "game" is half the battle—and indeed it is, when you're counting strokes in relation to par. When playing par golf, half the strokes are concerned with putting—two for each hole. But two-putt greens won't save the golfer who is having problems getting on the green. And most of the problems of getting to the green are involved with driving.

The importance of driving, and driving well, cannot be disclaimed. Drive badly and your whole game suffers. You're thrown off balance. You're affected mentally. You're susceptible to mistakes. But start off right, get a good drive long and straight, and your game will start jumping.

Careless play, with reference to driving, involves hitting the ball without giving thought to proper position for the following shot and failing to consider the hazards that are present. Good driving means knowing the course you are playing on, the position of the flag on each of the holes, and the presence of hazards, and fashioning your game accordingly.

If, for example, the pin is positioned to the left on a green, depending upon traps, the ideal position to aim your drive will be to the right, which ensures a better angle to come in to the flag and probably more green. Vice versa, of course, if the flag is positioned to the right on the green.

Naturally, no golfer is talented sufficiently to position his shot according to plan hole after hole. Everyone misses some of the time. But misses only call for additional planning and need not be cause for a disastrous or poorly played hole.

Imagine, for instance, that the flag is positioned to the left on a green—behind a trap—and that you drive to the left. Now you are facing a confined shot, over a trap, to hit to the flag. What should you do? It depends, of course, on a number of factors—the ability to hit the club that is needed, the amount of green that is playable for the shot, the condition of the green. But usually it is best to lay the ball up to a good position for the following shot. It's always good golf to avoid heroics—unless the hole means *win* or *lose*.

Plan each shot before teeing the ball. Know the best position to be in for the following shot. And if you miss that position, plan the next shot in relation to what follows or what should follow.

And be sure to plan with thought about hazards. Play away from trouble. Don't gamble too much unless you're adept at all facets of the game. You don't score birdies from the driving tee. Birdies result from approach shots following a good drive.

A good drive, of course, can "start" the moment you tee up the ball. It's seldom made clear, but there's a right place and a wrong place to tee up the ball. If you hook, for example, it's usually not good to tee up your ball on the right side of the teeing area. And if you slice, it's usually not good to tee up your ball on the left side. You're "losing" fairway, not taking advantage of the playable space. A basic plan is to tee up the ball where you have the best chance of making a golf shot that remains in play.

Consider what happens if you tee up the ball on the right side and hook the ball. Then consider what happens—the angle of the shot—if you tee up the ball from the left side and hook the ball. The latter, you'll find, has more fairway to "use" and hence is safer.

Of course, if you usually hit the ball straight, you can tee up the ball anywhere you wish.

Because of this thinking, I would naturally disagree with the theory of some that you tee up the ball on the side of trouble. It's only obvious: if there's trouble on the left and your tendency is to slice, you minimize your chances of staying in play if you tee up the ball on the left side. You'll escape the "trouble"—no doubt about that —but you'll also increase the chance of trouble on the right side. And your chances are slimmer of staying in play if you tee up the ball on the right side, with trouble on the right, if your tendency is to hook. You can prove the point by laying out a hole—or imagining a hole— and sketching the path of a hook or slice, draw or fade, from either side of the teeing ground.

Strategy off the tee also includes the length of the hole and the choice of clubs. Not always is it best to grab for the driver—to cite one thought—despite the fact that the hole may be long. You should use the club that will accomplish the task in the easiest way and the surest way. Fairway woods often should be used—even the irons—from off the tee. It depends upon conditions. The goal should be accuracy when you're driving on a hole, seldom distance.

A final thought is to learn to draw and fade the ball if you presently cannot. There are times when it's best to avoid a straight shot, and the draw or the fade is the only relief—on doglegs, for instance.

There is more to driving than meets the eye. Instead of just hitting, you should do some thinking and *play* the course. The rewards can be great.

draw and fade

by Jim Ferrier

Once you have overcome any tendency to hook or slice and have learned to hit the ball straight, you will find there are times when it's to your advantage not to hit it straight. With a dogleg on the right, for example, within driving distance, a slice can reduce the distance to the green and help your chances for a birdie. Similarly, with trees on the left, blocking a straight path to the green, a hook can solve the problem.

When deliberate and controlled, a slice is called a fade and a hook is called a draw. There are numerous situations which call for a draw or a fade. If there is trouble on the right, the draw can be used to play away from the trouble. If the wind is blowing from right to left, the fade can be used to nullify the effect of the wind on the ball. And on and on.

It's true that many golfers can play a reasonably good game without using these shots. But for those who desire to move steadily along—improve their game, take advantage of a course—these shots are needed.

*To produce a fade, use a weaker grip and assume an open stance
with the forward foot drawn back a bit from the normal position.
This will cause the clubhead to follow an outside-in path and
produce a sidespin on the ball that causes the desired left-to-
right slicing action.*

109

To produce a draw, use a stronger grip and assume a closed stance with your rear foot moved farther than normal away from the line to the target. This will cause the clubhead to follow an inside-out path and produce a sidespin on the ball that causes the desired right-to-left hooking action.

To produce a fade, an open stance must be used. That is, the left foot must be drawn back a couple of inches from the position it would be in with a square stance. The body is then aimed slightly to the left of its original position—square with the target. The clubface should be opened a little and the hands placed slightly ahead of their normal position with the right hand more on top and the left hand turned a little under.

The clubhead should be taken straight back from the ball, and the player should have the "feel" that the swing is more upright. On the downswing, the player should have the feel that the clubhead is traveling *through* the ball with a slight outside-in path in the swing which produces a fade spin.

To produce a slice, or an exaggerated fade, one needs merely to increase the mentioned changes in position, of course.

To produce a draw, opposite actions are needed. The right foot must be drawn back a couple of inches from the square position, and the body aimed to the right of the target to match the feet. And now, the left hand is more on top of the shaft and the right hand more underneath.

It's also necessary to employ a somewhat "flat" takeaway and the hands at the top of the swing should be in a lower position. The amount of draw or hook can be regulated by the flatness of the swing and the amount of roll-over of the hands at the moment of impact.

With both types of shots, it is important to have a good follow-through. The hands are important to both shots—in fading to cut across the line, and in drawing to roll over after coming to the ball from the inside path.

When hitting either a draw or a fade, it can also be helpful to play the ball back a couple of inches from its normal position.

backspin

by Ralph Guldahl

An approach shot that stops quickly once it hits the green is impressive to watch, and golfers who can accomplish this feat are envied by those who cannot.

High-handicap players believe that the shot is difficult and that some secret must be learned before they can expect to produce the shot on a consistent basis. The shot *is* difficult, but no secrets are involved. It can be executed by any player who is dedicated enough to learn the fundamentals of the shot and to practice it a lot.

It is often declared that backspin is produced by striking the ball cleanly and precisely about a quarter-inch above its base with a descending blow. This is correct—from a technical point of view. But I think this description can mislead a golfer, make him tend to "dive" at the ball on his downswing motion and hit it poorly.

The imparting of backspin, I think, can better be explained by describing a correct swing. Stop-action motion pictures show that while the backswing is still being completed, the good golfer's first move is a slight lateral shift of the hips forward, thus beginning a shift of the weight from the right side to the left side ahead of the downswing action. Pointedly, if there is one simple distinguishing move that separates the good golfer from the average golfer it is this lateral shift of the hips on the downswing. The point is that this move causes the forward motion which enables the golfer to "hit down and through" the ball, which imparts backspin and results in turf being taken after the ball has been hit.

We are all familiar with the bad results of not shifting the weight forward to the left side. Far too many golfers stay behind the ball with the majority of their weight on the right foot at impact, which causes a lifting up motion at the ball and loss of power and leverage.

It's true that almost every shot in golf, regardless of the club that is used, is hit with backspin, as the lofted clubface directs the blow below the ball's center of gravity rather than through the middle of the ball. Such action, of course, makes the bottom half of the ball spin forward and the upper half to spin in reverse. In other words, the ball spins forward on its underneath side and opposite, or backward, on its top side.

A fallacy connected with backspin is that the club must be swung in a way that will permit the face of the club to go "through" wide open—or looking skyward. There is an inherent danger to this idea. When an open clubface strikes the ball, there is a tendency to take the ball on the upward arc of the stroke. This, naturally, turns the shot into somewhat of a lob, which cannot be controlled consistently and eliminates the chance for the pinching action of the club against the ball which produces backspin.

Although backspin is applied mostly with pitching shots, it can be used when chipping too. When used for chipping, backspin is applied just as in pitching, by pinching the ball between the clubface and the ground at impact, which makes the ball take off very quickly and travel in a low trajectory. A ball which has been hit in this manner will hold its line well. The shot is particularly effective when the wind is blowing.

When hitting to produce backspin, the stance should be narrow and open, with the heels just a few inches apart on the shorter shots and just slightly wider apart on the longer shots. And the ball should be played off the right foot. Additionally, the left arm should be kept very straight throughout the stroke with the hands finishing well out in front and pointing toward the target. The length of the backswing should be determined by the length of the shot. For a very short shot, there is a minimum of backswing, and for a shot of maximum distance the backswing is normal.

Again, the ball must be struck with a descending stroke, but major thought should be given to the technical correctness of the swing. Remember the lateral shift to the left, and if the stroke is smooth and flowing and the ball struck sharply and crisply the loft of the club and its grooves will accomplish the mission.

the pitching wedge

by Eric Monti

The pitching wedge is probably the most often used iron. This is particularly true of single-figure players who have confidence in the club and can play more difficult shots than the average golfer. Regardless, the wedge can be a friend to the handicap golfer if only used for straightaway shots—pitch and chip shots and lofted chips.

Generally, the wedge can be used with accuracy from a maximum distance of 100 yards to a yard or two from the green. Some golfers, of course, hit wedges farther than others. The average player should not attempt to use it for more than 75 yards.

Mastery of the wedge requires a great deal of practice. You almost have to sleep with this club to master it. A good way to practice is to hit from an area 25 or 30 yards from the green, so you can discover through trial and error the amount of power it takes to get the ball where it's supposed to go. Gradually the distance can be increased until you reach your maximum distance. If you try to push the wedge too far you can expect a lot of trouble.

115

Short pitch shots with the wedge demand a short backswing and follow-through, with very little shift of weight to the right on the backswing. A strong left side is essential.

The vital statistics of the wedge are simple. Normally, the club has three or four degrees more loft than a 9-iron, and it's about half an inch shorter in shaft length and somewhat heavier. Usually there is about one-fourth of an ounce difference in weight between the consecutive irons. That is, a 5-iron is usually about one-fourth of an ounce heavier than a 4-iron and a 4-iron about one-fourth of an ounce heavier than a 3-iron. But the pitching wedge is normally about an ounce heavier than a 9-iron. The heavier weight permits a player to use the wedge with less than a full swing and therefore aids in accuracy.

The greatest difference between the wedge and the other clubs is in its sole. The wedge has what is called a flanged sole. The flanged sole ensures that the club will not dig into the turf too deeply, as a 9-iron might. As a result, the player using a wedge has an extra margin of safety—insurance that the club will not lose its speed when it contacts the turf.

Basic to good wedge play is a good grip. Without a good grip, you cannot expect to play a good shot with the wedge—or any other club, for that matter. A somewhat light grip is recommended for this club, but it should be held firmly in the last three fingers of the left hand to prevent it from turning when it hits the turf.

With the wedge, you must get the ball up in the air quickly and have it stop quickly when it lands. To do so you must plan the shot—if a full wedge—from a slightly open stance, the ball just forward of the middle of the stance. As the shot becomes shorter, a slightly more open stance is used, the right foot being moved even more toward the ball.

For the full wedge shot, you should have about 60 percent of your weight on the left foot at address. Then you should use the same swing that you use with the 9-iron or an 8-iron. This means that you should shift your weight to the right and then back again to the left, with a full body turn. The club is taken back the maximum distance consistent with control, as with any other club. However, the shorter length of the wedge and the open stance automatically shortens the length of the backswing.

As the wedge shot becomes progressively shorter, you should put additional weight on your left side at address and shift less weight to the right on the backswing. When you get down to about

For a full wedge shot, about 60 percent of the weight should be on the left foot at address, and the ball should be played in the middle of the stance. The hands should be ahead of the club-head, and fairly close to the body.

The weight should be shifted to the right, then back to the left with a full body turn for the full wedge shot. The club should be taken back the maximum distance consistent with control, as with any club.

a 15-yard pitch, you should not shift your weight at all. Instead, you should use your arms, hands, and wrists to make the shot. And you should choke down on the club until the right hand is almost touching the steel shaft.

Perhaps the most difficult of all wedge shots is the "cut shot." The cut shot should be used when, for one reason or another, you must make the ball rise quickly and on an extremely steep angle. For instance, your ball has come to rest just ten yards off the green, but a tall, thick hedge stands midway between you and the putting surface. There is no way to go under, around, or through the obstacle. You must hit a shot that will climb rapidly, clear the hedge, and quickly come to rest on the green. Your only solution is the cut shot.

The cut shot is played by opening the blade of the club and opening the stance. This will cause the clubhead to move into the ball from outside the intended line of flight, cutting under the ball and imparting clockwise, or slice spin. If played correctly the shot will stop just as quickly as it rises.

The cut shot is a difficult stroke to master, but with practice it can become an important addition to your shotmaking repertoire.

weather

by Dan Murphy

Few golfers would deny that weather conditions affect a golfer's play. Wind, especially, is annoying to most golfers, and rain and cold can be just as bad.

In the 1972 Sahara Invitational, for instance, when the golfers were fighting a strong wind and cold weather, the scores soared. The cutoff score was 151—9 over par. And in the 1972 U.S. Open at Pebble Beach, fourteen of the sixteen leading finishers, fighting wind and hard greens, shot 75 or higher.

When playing in bad weather, you will be sure to have more problems than normally. To meet these problems, you must alter your style and strategy.

Let's say, for example, that pitching to the green is your favorite shot—and usually successful. Under ordinary conditions you would hit this shot with your pitching wedge and stop it very close to the flag. But with a strong wind blowing against you, there is a great chance that your shot will go wild or come up short. It is therefore good judgment to hit the ball in a way that will keep it low and diminish the chances of the wind taking it off course or causing it to come up short.

To play in the wind a golfer just has to alter his strategy. Two of the most essential rules for a golfer to remember when the flags start flying is to choose the right club and to swing easy at the ball. Other adjustments must be made according to whether you are hitting against the wind, with the wind, or across the wind.

When playing in a headwind, you can be sure you won't get as much yardage as you do in normal conditions. Should you try to get more yardage you will only succeed in blowing the round.

Naturally, it's impossible to say how much yardage you will lose in a given situation. But it's a good bet that you can lose as much as 20 yards in a wind that is blowing approximately 20 miles per hour. And you can lose as much as 40 yards in a really strong wind.

Common sense therefore dictates that you should make an attempt to keep the ball low when the wind is blowing against you. To do this, you usually use one club more. If a shot would normally call for a 7-iron, you use a 6-iron, and if a shot would normally call for a 5-iron, you use a 4-iron. This will decrease the loft of the ball and increase your distance.

Under average wind conditions, one more club is enough. There are always exceptions, of course. On the spectacular par-3 16th hole at Cypress Point, for instance, a good golfer can use anything from a 4-iron to a driver for the hole, depending upon the fierceness of the wind.

The biggest mistake made by the majority of golfers when playing against the wind is to try to compensate by swinging harder than normal. Such an action, of course, will force you out of your normal groove and multiply the problems. And when you swing too hard, there's an extreme danger of "scooping" the ball or hitting it higher into the wind. Just use a smooth, easy swing.

Also important when hitting into the wind is to play the ball back an inch or two from the normal position to ensure a low flight, and to put more weight than normal on the left foot at address and keep it there throughout the swing. You might take a wider stance to help your balance.

124

If you have a tendency to hook or slice, a headwind will magnify either of these problems to atrocious size. Contrarily, a following wind usually tends to straighten out hooks and slices and add to accuracy. Although a following wind will normally add distance to your shots, a great many golfers have a greedy tendency to try for more distance than is warranted in a following wind. As a result, they usually overswing and get a poor shot. So the injunction to swing easy applies to a following wind as well as a headwind.

As for clubs to use in a following wind, general procedure dictates one club less than normal. On a normal 4-iron shot, for instance, use a 5-iron. The result is greater loft and therefore greater distance.

When hitting with the wind behind you, take a sturdy stance, perhaps a little wider, and play the ball an inch or so forward of your normal position. You might tee the ball a little higher to take advantage of the wind.

With a crosswind it's likely that you will get less distance from your shots and lose accuracy as well. So it's a good procedure to use one more club than you normally would and allow for the drift by hitting into the wind a bit. In other words, if the wind is blowing from left to right, aim somewhat left of the target—just slightly if the wind is not too strong, and more if the wind is stronger.

And be careful where you tee up the ball. There is sometimes an advantage to teeing the ball in a particular spot. If the wind is blowing from left to right, for example, and there is trouble on the right, it's usually advantageous to tee the ball up on the right side of the teeing area and give yourself more target in the trouble-free area.

When playing into a quartering wind—one that blows at an angle—there is little you can do to improve your chances for success, with the exception, perhaps, of electing to use one club more. In a quartering wind, you have to guess how much to allow.

In summary, then: when playing in a wind, regardless of the type, analyze carefully its force and direction and allow for these when you choose your club and remember always to swing easy at the ball.

When playing in the rain, it's extremely important to maintain a firm grip and to select your clubs with the greatest care.

Wet hands or a wet club, besides causing slippage, can also give you a feeling of insecurity and affect all parts of your swing. Naturally, you can do very little about wet hands or a wet grip except to wipe them before playing a shot (carry a towel hung under your umbrella), but you can gain ground by choosing your clubs correctly.

It's accepted that you will get less distance in wet weather, so an important point is to use one club more than you normally would to minimize the loss of distance. Exceptions could be long iron shots and fairway shots. Many good golfers feel that it's easier—and safer—to use a 4-wood, for example, than a 2-iron off the fairway, or a 4-wood instead of a 2-or 3-wood. A 4-wood will get the ball in the air much more easily. You can expect very little roll on the wet grass.

Similarly, it's sometimes advantageous to use one club less than normal when using the short irons. A clubhead striking a wet ball in wet grass will impart little spin to the ball, so it will go farther than normal.

In this connection, it's far better to chip instead of pitch when near the green. It's easier to judge distance with a chip from wet grass than a pitch. And accuracy is improved.

Two essentials which should be considered when hitting off wet grass are to hit the ball more cleanly than you normally would and to keep your feet planted firmly. It's easy to slip in wet grass.

Playing from wet sand is another problem that demands some thought. There are two methods of recovering from a wet sand trap, and each is dictated by the lie of the ball. If the ball is buried in the sand, you should address the ball with an open clubface, with your weight largely on the left side. You should lift the club somewhat abruptly on the backswing and try to penetrate the sand about four inches behind the ball. Only practice will tell you how hard you should swing the club.

If the ball is lying cleanly in the sand, your method of recovery will be dictated by the nature of the sand. If it is soggy, you should play the shot with your sand wedge. If it is hard, you should play the shot with your pitching wedge, since the sharper blade will dig into the sand more easily.

If you have an extremely sloppy lie, it's usually best to chip the ball out, using the club you prefer for the shot. But when doing this, it is important to hit the ball first with a descending stroke. And like any chip shot, an open stance should be used with the weight largely on the left leg.

Putting can be troublesome too. Naturally, when the green is soggy you will have to stroke the ball firmer to overcome the drag which is caused by the water. And you will have to putt straighter to the hole, as the wetness minimizes the normal break. But while you must hit the ball harder than normal, avoid lengthening the stroke, as this will cause you to waver off line. Instead, just increase the force of the blow.

A final thought: check the face of your club before a stroke to see that it's free of grass, which can deaden the putt and cause it to be short or off line.

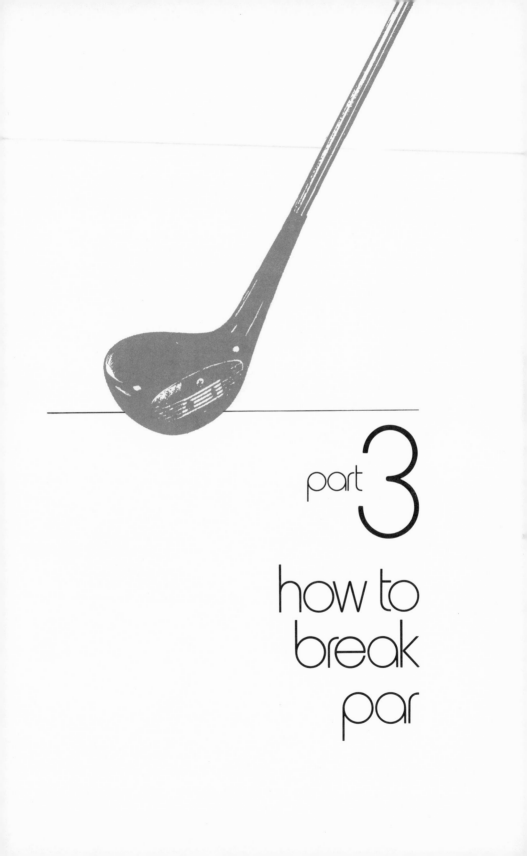

part 3

how to
break
par

getting down to scratch

20

Most people playing golf today started the game relatively late in life. If you're among them and you still aspire to shooting in the 70s and sometimes breaking par, you have your work cut out for you. For most low-handicap players learned their golf as youngsters. Their good swing habits were learned early through imitation. And since their basic swing patterns are ingrained, they require little conscious thought about the mechanics of the swing during actual play. This leaves the mind free to concentrate on playing strategy and other factors.

But whether you started as a youngster or an adult, shooting scratch golf requires more than just a good golf swing. It takes a complete golf game and a lot of finesse. You must be able to fade or draw the ball, and know when it's advisable to do either. You must master every conceivable type of trouble shot. For if you're human, you'll find yourself "in jail" just like the big stars who occasionally knock one into the jungle, too. You must know how to feather a long

131

iron shot or drill a low-flying 1-iron under the wind. And learn the punch, or push shot, for cheating the elements on windy days.

However, you could have all these skills and still not be a par-buster.

Most of the golfers who hold PGA playing cards have the necessary skills to win a money event on the tour. Watch their finely tuned swings on the practice tee. If you didn't know their names, it would be hard to pick a winner. Yet, some are up on the big score-board for a sizable prize check every week, and others with equal skills are left at the post when the money is handed out. What spells the difference? What separates the men from the boys?

The difference between the golf star and the also-ran hinges as much as anything on *mental approach,* the proper use of gray matter. Desire, application, concentration, judgment, equilib-rium, poise, confidence, and a competitive spirit—these are the factors that make a champion. And they're the factors that can help you break par.

Ben Hogan came back from a bone-crushing, near-fatal accident to win three more U.S. Open Championships. That's desire. Lee Trevino pounded out 600 practice balls a day on his way up to national prominence and two U.S. Opens. That's application. Jack Nicklaus plotted beforehand every distance and every shot in the rounds that he would play to win three National Opens. That's judg-ment. Arnold Palmer vowed he'd drive the first green of the 360-yard 1st hole of the Cherry Hills course at Denver in the 1960 Open. He did it on the final day. He missed his eagle, but got the birdie to start him on a record-breaking score of 30-35 to edge out Jack Nicklaus for the title. That's confidence. And who can forget Gary Player's poise and concentration when he was threatened by anti-Apartheid pickets at a major tournament a few years ago?

The ability to play well under pressure can only be ac-quired by doing it frequently. If you play friendly games that get you around in par figures, the cool, serious atmosphere of a tourna-ment can come as a shock. It can cause you to tense up and try too hard. And that's when the bogies mount.

A certain amount of a keyed-up feeling for a tournament is an asset. Too much of it is a hazard. Good physical condition can help you free yourself of tension. That's one reason golfers such as

Gary Player, Lee Trevino, and Jim Jamieson have taken to jogging. They know the mind is less apt to boggle when the legs and heart are strong. And they also realize, through experience, that when the legs are weak the coordination of the swing falls apart.

Perceptive judgment, too, is born of experience. The smart par shooter is a sharp observer. For example, from the moment he hits his first practice balls before teeing off he checks the wind direction and the feeling of the pressure in the air. Is the air heavy and moist, or light and airy? Either will affect the flight of the ball. Will he have to hit the ball low today to keep it in play, or quarter it into the wind?

From his practice rounds on the course he already knows on which holes he'll have to fade or draw his tee shots. He's made notes of points of reference for gauging distance, things like a certain bush, tree, or trap. As he plays one hole, he'll glance at any adjoining holes to see if he can spot the pin placement on the remaining holes to be played. He checks the texture and speed of the putting surface as soon as he reaches the green. He observes the speed and line of any putters who stroke the ball before he does.

The astute player uses good judgment in his decisions to gamble or play safe. He never tries the impossible shot in medal play; it might be too costly if it doesn't come off. In match play, he may take a chance, since the most he can lose is the hole and not the tournament.

Above all, the seasoned scratch player maintains his rhythm, from the moment he starts for the course to the time he completes play. He knows that if he is rushed unduly, or slowed down, he'll lose the natural rhythm of his golf swing. And when he loses that, his timing goes. And this calamitous loss could lead to an upset of his poise and confidence. By the way, no one ever hurried Walter Hagen or Jack Nicklaus.

So, if you're out to break par, pay special heed to the mental side of golf. The mind affects the nerves and body. And conversely, the condition of the body affects your thinking. So stay in shape, and you'll stay alert to every positive factor this great game of golf demands.

strong
left
side

by Labron Harris

If you don't have a good left side and strong, fast hands, you have very little chance of breaking par. Many people wonder how Chi Chi Rodriguez, who looks as if a strong wind might blow him away, can hit the ball as far as Arnold Palmer, who is about fifty pounds heavier and very muscular. Chi Chi offsets his small stature by using his left side, legs, and hands with greater speed on the downswing.

One of the best exercises to strengthen the left side is simply to swing a club smoothly with the left hand only. Start out with about a dozen swings and then gradually increase the exercise until you can do fifty each day. Or while watching TV or just sitting in a chair, extend your left arm even with your Adam's apple, push the left hand and arm back toward the right shoulder until the left shoulder touches the chin, and then pull the left hand and arm back past the chin. This will not only strengthen and stretch the left side but will develop muscle memory.

To strengthen the hands and forearms, roll up a soft towel and grip it with both hands about six inches apart. Extend the arms in front of you and rotate the right hand toward you and the left away, as if you were wringing water out of it. Later, rotate in the opposite direction. Another good exercise is to extend the arms to the side shoulder-high, close the hands, and twist or rotate the hands and arms back and forth. This can be done with or without a light weight. These last two exercises will strengthen your hands, wrists, and forearms.

To strengthen the legs, do deep knee bends slowly, holding the hands on the knee caps to help support the cartilage, and run in place, jog, or ride a bicycle.

A great exercise to stretch all the muscles in a smooth, rhythmic manner is to stand up fairly tall, then sit back so that the weight is toward the heels and extend the left hand and arm as if you were gripping a golf club. Extend the right hand and softly grip the left wrist. Your right elbow will be pointing to the right hip. Now turn the left shoulder until it reaches the chin. Hold the head as still as possible and keep the left heel on the ground. This exercise will stretch your muscles from the left hand, arm, shoulder, back, and leg muscles. Do it slowly and as smoothly as possible. This is great for making the whole body flexible. If at first you can't turn your left shoulder all the way to the chin, go as far as you can, and as you practice it the muscles will slowly become more flexible, giving you a bigger turn and more power.

Remember, if you want to shoot par or better you have to hit the ball well over 200 yards or you will never reach the 450-yard par-4 in two. You have to be able to reach the long par-4s in regulation and once in a while get on the long par-5s in two. Remember, power comes from muscles coiling and stretching, and without proper exercises you can't have either. So work on these exercises. Correct practice makes perfect.

When I practice for a tournament, I always work on what I call key fundamentals. I always check my grip first, making sure my hands are square to each other. Because I have fairly large hands, I use a palm grip in the left hand with my thumb on top of the shaft, and the V formed by the thumb and forefinger points to my chin. My right hand is more of a finger grip, with the thumb and forefinger forming a V that points toward my right shoulder. My grip pressure is medium firm in the left hand and fairly light in the right.

After I am satisfied with my grip, I check my stance and balance. I want my heels to be fairly square to each other with my right foot and toe square and my left toe slightly open. Weight is back toward the heels. Now that I feel comfortable with my grip and stance I will really get to work on the rhythm or tempo of my backswing. To anyone who wants to play par golf this is an absolute must. You just cannot have too smooth a backswing. Another key factor in playing par golf is working on keeping the head as still as possible.

There are many different ways to start the downswing. I like to concentrate on just one—pulling the left hand down and through the ball. Over the years I have worked hard on this left-side action and it does the job for me. There are many golfers whose right shoulder won't stay in position on the downswing, so they use different methods of starting the downswing. Some concentrate on pushing down with the left heel. Others feel that they get good results with the left knee making the first move. Some of the top players claim the left hip is their key. And there are others who feel that they get their best results by concentrating on pushing off the right foot and leg—it helps them keep the right side under control.

Whatever method is used to start the downswing, the left hand must be the guide through the ball.

I know one thing for sure. I have never seen, nor do I expect to see, anyone play par golf who lets the right shoulder, right elbow, or right hand get out of control until the ball has left the clubhead. I have been fortunate enough to help many good golfers shoot par golf, and some of them varied their methods depending on their particular mannerisms. But the four basic keys to par golf are a good grip; starting from a well-balanced position; good rhythm or tempo; and keeping the left side in control.

It seems that one of the hardest fundamentals to get across to advanced players who want to shoot par golf is to swing within themselves. I recall that when I first started to play on the tour I was terribly proud about how long I could hit my drives and how far I could hit my irons. However, when I started playing with great swingers like Sam Snead, Julius Boros, and Gene Littler, I began to realize that they seemed to hit the ball just about the same distance as I did but they controlled it much better and were winning more tournaments. As I watched and studied them I began to realize that they were working well within themselves while I was letting everything go on all of my swings. I began to smooth out my swing and try to feel that I was swinging at about 75 percent of my maximum power, and to my amazement I lost very little distance and became much more accurate. I now realize that as I smoothed out my swing all my muscles, both large and small, could coordinate well within this rhythmic action, giving me the same power as I had before but with much more control. Now, fifteen years later, I see that Sam Snead, at sixty, or thereabouts, and Julius Boros at fifty-four, are still playing super golf. I am convinced that swinging within oneself is an important factor in the longevity of many great players.

mental approach

by Mortie Dutra

There's more to playing golf than the physical process of hitting a golf ball. And there's to breaking 90, 80, or par than having a good swing, a knowledge of the clubs, and familiarity with the course being played. Equally important is a positive mental approach. Think negatively while playing golf and you'll make mistakes. Think positively and you'll get better scores than your physical capabilities alone would earn you.

What goes on in your head is just as important as a good physical swing. Golf, in the final analysis, is a psychological game.

Strangely, a great many golfers subconsciously fight the idea that they're going to be good, that they're going to make a par or shoot a low score. This perverse "will to fail" haunts everyone at times, some more than others, and must be fought with positive thinking. Too often a golfer will look around and see only problems— trouble spots. At all times, it is necessary to shut off your mind from all outside agencies.

It is plainly evident—at least to me—that once you have mastered the rudiments of the game, the key to improvement is in thinking better. If you think correctly, you're on your way to a respectable score, according to your talent. If you think incorrectly—let negative thoughts and feelings run rampant in your mind—you're headed for failure.

Walter Hagen, one of the immortals of golf, agreed. "Golf is loaded with guys who can hit the ball a mile, but few of them ever win because they don't know how to think."

Hagen once told me that he was prepared even if he missed a half-dozen shots. "I never know at what stage of the game it might happen, but I'm always prepared." Hagen had a great ability to think correctly, and this was one of the reasons he was such a strategist on the golf course.

Confidence is the greatest single ally that a golfer can have. But confidence won't result just from wanting to be confident. This sought-after quality usually results from hitting some good drives, making some excellent approaches, or sinking some tricky putts. Or making a good shot from the sand that settles near the cup, or a string of two or three pars.

You cannot, of course, simply decide to hole some long putts or sink a sand shot and expect to succeed. You can, however, increase your chances of making the putts, or the sand shot, by thinking correctly, thinking that you can.

The time to begin this mental preparation is right at the start of a particular round, at the first hole. First you should think, "I'm going to make a par." Then you should think that your drive is going straight or to an area of the fairway that you've picked as a target. And *believe* that it will!

Don't think about the things that could possibly go wrong or the apparent hazards. Don't say to yourself, "I'll probably slice so I'll aim to the left," or, "I've got to stay clear of those trees on the right." Just think success. Erase the thoughts that are obviously negative and rob so many golfers of whatever chance they had to succeed. By staying busy, figuring out ways to make a good shot, you can eliminate ways (or thoughts, as it were) of doing it poorly.

Don't let your mind wander and conjure up problems that might develop should you miss a shot, hit into the woods or into a bunker. Once you have planned your route to the pin, think about the shot you are about to make and eradicate thoughts about later shots. Keep your mind in the present.

Sure it's difficult to concentrate for 18 holes. Even some pros say that if they are not careful they fall asleep mentally after about 12 holes. The right kind of concentration takes training. So force yourself at every hole to keep concentrating and thinking about all the good shots you want to hit.

An additional "don't" is don't hit a shot before swinging the club. If, for example, you have hit a good drive and your second shot is somewhat easy, don't tell yourself what a terrible thing it would be to flub the approach shot and the chance for a birdie. Instead, think, "I'm going to get close and one-putt this hole." You're instilling the thought of success into your mind, and your mind, when thinking positively, will direct your body to produce it.

Similarly, if an opponent makes a long drive and yours falls shorter, don't let it throw you. Just concentrate harder on the next shot with the thought in mind that you'll even the score. Concentrate on your own game 100 percent of the time.

An excellent example of positive thinking is Billy Casper, an all-time great in the world of golf. He wastes no time when he approaches his ball. He knows before address what he's going to do or wants to do. He's prepared mentally, and he hits automatically without worry of result. Most often, it's good. Trevino is the same way. Gene Sarazen was also this type.

It has often been said that more important than good form is a clear mental picture of what is to happen. Most of the pros have flaws in their form which result in a bad shot occasionally, but they manage to shoot good most of the time because of confidence. They can see the ball go where they want it to go before they swing. Their subconscious minds and their nervous systems take over at the start and direct their muscles.

Another great player who exudes confidence—positive thinking—is Arnold Palmer. From the moment he prepares to begin a round until the round is finished he's a picture of dynamic confidence and deliberate playing. He lines up his shot, fashions his grip, addresses the ball, then hits with the thought that the shot will be good.

140

Confidence is his forte—proved by the fact that his numerous "charges" have met with success. When he fades the ball from behind a tree, he *knows* he can make it. He doesn't think *miss*. When he was stroking those winning putts he wasn't hoping they would drop; he knew they would.

If all you see is the rough, nine times out of ten that's where your ball will go. One should only think of mechanics on the practice tee—on the golf course trust what you've learned and concentrate on scoring.

Good imagination put to use in the right way will make you score better even if your swing is not going the way you want it to. Psychologically, if a golfer, even a pro, feels he cannot pull off a particular shot he usually won't.

If you think you will miss, you probably will. Your mind is a very impressionable instrument. If you seek out reasons to miss a shot, your mind will usually oblige. You must feel that each shot is a makable shot, then apply what talent you happen to have and accept the result. If it's good—fine. If it's poor, forget it. Or at least don't permit it to affect your play.

As they say on the pro trail, "Playing in a game where just a little bad break can make a big difference, you've got to forget what is behind you or go crazy." Patty Berg concurs: "You've got to forget that double bogey as you walk to the next hole. If for one instant you let your concentration and confidence falter, you're dead."

Many golfers, of course, cannot equal the positive thinking practiced by a Casper, Palmer, Nicklaus, Hogan, or Hagen. But most golfers, if they want to, can think positively enough to convince themselves that the upcoming shot will be right on the mark.

Many golfers who are presently scoring in the 70s could be beating par without much trouble just by altering their thinking, gaining confidence. It's not unusual for a golfer to say, "I'm really unlucky. Whatever I attempt, it turns out bad." Or "I can't improve." Or "I'm little better than I was when I started." Or "Rest assured, if there's sand on the course, I'm sure to find it." These players are beaten before they start. To do well consistently, you must want to do well and believe in yourself.

There's no doubt about it—positive thinking is an enormous asset to a serious golfer, regardless of his talent. There are examples without end to prove this thought.

Often a player who shoots in the 70s most of the time is heard to say, "I'm doing all right; I'm holding my average." You can bet he will continue to shoot above par until he changes his attitude. Many golfers are doomed to mediocrity simply because they don't have the vision or desire to do better.

A place where confidence particulary pays off is on the green. Often a player who is facing a long putt will say to himself, "I'll try and get close and two-putt this hole." More positive and more helpful would be the thought, "I'm going to hole out." Such an attitude will sink more putts than merely trying to get close.

Similarly, many players who are facing a short chip after a couple of shots on a par-4 hole will say to themselves, "I've got to get close and one-putt this green to get my par." Better if they would think, "I can sink this shot and get a birdie."

It cannot be denied, on the other hand, that confidence and ability must go together. It's easier to think strongly that you'll make a shot if you're in a habit of making the shot which poses the challenge. And it's not so easy to be bubbling with confidence when you're facing a shot that's new to you or extremely difficult. But give it a try. Think there's a chance. You'll be surprised how often it will turn out well simply if you think it will.

But remember that confidence—positive thinking—isn't kidding yourself that you're better than you are. Confidence is making the most of your talent, whatever it is.

playing
under
pressure

by John Mahaffey

When you're playing competitive golf and have an important shot to make, it's only natural to feel the pressure and become tense at times. In every big-time tournament pressure takes its toll, even among the biggest stars. Sometimes it's noticeable and sometimes it's not.

A classic example occurred in the 1966 U.S. Open, when Arnold Palmer had a seven-stroke lead with but nine holes remaining and lost the tournament. Most people who were watching felt that he was feeling the pressure and couldn't fight it off.

More recently, Judy Rankin, the Ladies Professional Golf Association star, went into the final round of the 1972 Winner's Circle tournament with a two-stroke lead and then ballooned to a 77 and lost the event by three strokes. She three-putted four holes in the final round, hardly her usual type of play.

There are thousands of incidents of golfers being beaten by pressure—or tension. They occur in every tournament. More often than not, when Jack Nicklaus, Palmer, or any of the other touring professionals misses a short putt, pressure is really to blame. They know how to putt; they make few technical mistakes.

The ordinary golfer, of course, doesn't have to face the pressure that accompanies a professional tournament. But almost every golfer who is knocking on the door of par has numerous occasions to feel the pressure—whether in a tournament or while playing for a couple of dollars. He wants to win—for money or prestige.

Quite often championships are won by the players who can handle the pressure the best, rather than by those who are most expert at the technical skills of the game. There are, to be sure, differences in the playing ability of the touring players, but they are relatively slight, despite the fact that some players consistently score better than other players. Much of the difference often results from pressure. It is the player who can handle the pressure who usually scores best.

There are numerous causes of pressure. Some of the most prevalent are: looking back, looking too far ahead, thinking about failure, and thinking about winning.

Many players have difficulty in erasing the thoughts of a disastrous hole—or even a bogey. But seldom can a player improve his play by looking back or thinking about problems while he's still playing. There is nothing you can do about a hole that has already been played. You must play one hole at a time, and the one to play is the one you are facing.

Of course, you should consider your mistakes and mentally isolate the causes for the mistakes. You should not, however, be thinking about the past when you're facing the future.

Looking too far ahead is another mistake. As previously stated, you should play one hole at a time. If you are thinking about a hole other than the one you are playing, you're jeopardizing success.

Thinking about failure is equally bad. Gary Player wrote in his book, *Gary Player's Golf Secrets*, "Tension comes from fear of failure. . . . You can bring on tension by thinking about catching a trap, hitting out of bounds or missing a putt."

You can also bring on tension by thinking about losing. And many golfers, including professionals, often do this.

As bad, perhaps, is thinking about winning. If you're thinking about winning—an event or a bet—your mind is wandering. You can hardly play at your best if you're mentally accepting a trophy or collecting a bet you have not yet won.

It is also disastrous to put a premium on winning. Every golfer wants to win, and positive thinking is an asset—but by concentrating only on winning you're bound to get jumpy when something unlucky happens or you make a bad shot.

There are ways to control pressure. One is to concentrate entirely on planning and executing shots.

Another way is to slow up your pace—swing slower and putt slower. And another is to stabilize your pace.

Player's remedy is "to direct my thinking toward making a good shot. I visualize how a good shot will feel and look. Then I give it my best."

One more remedy is never to talk about golf, or think about the game, when away from the course. Do your thinking when it comes.

Such "remedies" can't apply to everyone, of course. Each golfer, naturally, is an individual. And what will work to relieve tension for one may not work for another. It is up to each player to perfect a method which works best for him.

But better than a "remedy" for pressure or tension is elimination of the cause. At any rate, a golfer who can handle pressure, or feels no pressure, is certain to be a better player and a player who is capable of going all the way in the game.

head
position

by Rafe Botts

One dictionary definition of "head" is "the foremost part of a thing." Most great golfers will agree with this thinking, at least in essence. In the game they play, the head is definitely the foremost part. Whether it be in the placement of it or the thinking it does, that area above the shoulders is the computer that programs your game and often produces a variety of results.

A careful study of great golfers like Byron Nelson, Ralph Guldahl, Bobby Jones, and others of their stature shows that they anchored their swings with a rigid head position. They seldom moved their heads perceptibly during a shot. In the vernacular, they stayed "over the ball." Their bodies moved "around" the head.

As a consequence, the professional golfers of the era of those mentioned were noticeably very accurate with their shots. Today, it's somewhat different. Emphasis is on the long ball, and the power hitter is making his move.

This is probably the major reason why many of the professionals are often hitting from the rough or from behind a tree on the finishing holes. The quest is for distance, and direction has become secondary.

This preoccupation with distance may have been caused by the plethora of outstanding golfers presently playing on the tour. In the 1930s and 40s, the professional tour was not nearly as competitive as it is today. The presence of the tour "rabbits" who can have four hot rounds in any given week has put the premium on distance in professional golf. Accuracy is fine, but only if it accompanies the big blow—that seems to be the philosophy. There is little doubt that approaching a green with a medium or short iron sets up more birdies than a long iron, but when the tee shot goes far astray the option appears in a different light.

Many of today's golfers live by the dictum "You can learn to be accurate, but you can't learn to be long." As a result, they let fly from the teeing area and put a great deal of faith in their ability to swing the driver.

There is certainly more than one reason why a golfer slices, hooks, tops, or does whatever else he does wrong. But, by process of elimination, the cause may be detected.

There is an axiom that states, "Wherever the head goes, the body will follow." You see this in a gymnast's reverse flip or a diver's somersault routine. Have you ever been driving down a street looking to the left and suddenly discovered that you have unwittingly been steering in that direction? It is all because of the head. In acrobatic routines, the head position is all-important. It dictates the movements of the rest of the body. In golf, it assumes as much relative importance, but its role is often misunderstood or taken too literally.

The first things a novice hears about golf is to "keep your head down" or "keep it still." The spirit, not the letter, of those words should be heeded. It is virtually impossible to hit a golf ball well with your head "down" at all times. It is restrictive to hit it well with your head "still" at all times.

What the better players are doing, of course, is moving off the ball slightly during the backswing and then moving back onto it during the downswing. Magnificent timing is required to return yourself to the original address position. For all practical purposes, only very talented players can do this and still play well. For them it is simply a matter of doing it often enough to get accustomed to it, and this means playing nearly every day.

If you are sliding off the ball with your head, say, four inches on your backswing, then your body is moving off the ball that same amount. In order to get back into the proper position to be able to strike the ball properly, you have to slide back through the same amount at exactly the right time.

But this is the way most of the players on the tour hit the ball today. Consequently, they hit it farther and a little less consistently than they would like. This is one reason you have so many new names popping up each week as high-finishers. Someone will get hot one week and hit the ball very well, but then you won't hear from him for another six or eight months.

It should be kept in mind, though, that moving off the ball like this is only for the established player who can maneuver and control his body to such an extent that the lateral movement becomes an integral part of his swing. Even for low-handicap players lateral movement should be held to a minimum. An effort should be made to keep the head and shoulders behind the ball throughout the swing. On the follow-through, the head should be allowed to follow the flight of the ball. If an attempt is made to remain over the ball into the follow-through, the swing will be restricted and anything is liable to happen. The force of the arms and club will and should pull the head up, but only after contact is made.

If the head leaks to a position in front of the ball before contact or during the downswing, there is no way solid contact can be made. More than likely the golfer will slice from this position. More than 85 percent of all golfers slice the ball, so obviously more thought should go into the role the head plays.

The principles of head movement apply not only to the tee shot, either, but to all facets of the game. In putting and chipping, however, the head cannot be allowed to move at all. This might be extended to include any approach shot where accuracy is paramount. You can get away with some head movement and body sway with the driver and long irons, but when you must place your shot in a particular area on the green, the head must not move off the ball.

Chipping, pitching, and putting are the real precision shots in golf, and any unnecessary movements of the head and body will only lead to frustration and added strokes.

The whole key to the game, with the head as its focal point, is balance. If a golfer who can swing a club with any degree of ability at all addresses the ball consistently in a sound position and in balance, he will rarely hit the ball very far off line. As long as a golfer can make a move away from the ball with his head in position, turn around the head, and strike the ball with the head still in position, coming up only after contact has been made, he is in pretty good shape. Then it is just a matter of polishing techniques.

flying
elbows

by Ron Taylor

Low-handicap golfers are not immune to that malady called "flying elbows." As a result, many golfers who have achieved a good leg and hip movement are still not hitting the ball straight consistently. Pointedly, they use their hands excessively. They are uncocking too soon or trying to deliver the hit with their hands.

Ben Hogan found that he had a greater degree of accuracy in his golf swing when he practiced with his elbows strapped together. And Hogan was never known to waste time on his golf swing, so he must have had the knowledge that the use of roll of the elbows is one of the most important parts of the swing.

A check of the elbow position of professional golfers at address position shows that they vary to some degree, but in most instances the elbows are facing the body and are in close—inside both hips.

Flying elbows are the result of taking the club away on the backswing with the hands. Using the hands too much in this man-

150

ner, both in the backswing and downswing, will cause inaccurate shots. If the hands are too quick, they will roll over and close the clubface and thus pull the ball to the left. If the hands remain locked, the clubface will be open and the ball will be hit to the right.

The cure for flying elbows is to make an effort to keep both elbows in close to the body at address, inside both hips. Just how close will depend upon the individual—how he is built and what feels comfortable and natural to him. The right elbow should be pointing to the right hip, not only at address but through the entire backswing. If this is done, there is no way the elbow will fly in the swing.

There is a definite relationship between the right elbow and the hip movement. This is all part of the term "one-piece" swing. The right elbow doesn't move away from the right hip. The elbow stays in close to the body as a quarter-turn of the hip is made on the backswing. There should be no tension, and it should not be forced to stay there as you allow it to fold and point to the ground.

If the right elbow points behind the right shoulder, you have taken the club back with the hands. Try to retain the feeling of keeping the right elbow in close to the body all the way to the top of the backswing, even though the left arm is remaining straight. Try to visualize both elbows still pointing to the ground. While at the top of the backswing and getting ready to come down, the legs will motivate the hips out of the way and you should allow the hands and arms to drop or slide down while the hips are in motion. Now and only now can you hit down through the ball without turning the top of your body. If you make the movement with the hands at the top of the backswing, you are going to go to the outside because the body is turning away. As you go through the ball at impact, the right elbow stays close to the body and the left hip is turning ahead of the left arm but the arm is not really moving away from the hip.

Just beyond impact, the hip is turned approximately six to eight inches away from the elbow, which is still facing down and facing the hip. It is important to keep both elbows as close to the body as possible at this point. Let the forearms and hands go, but keep the elbows close to the body.

The backswing and downswing should be a coordinated movement—legs, hips, arms, shoulders, and hands; no one moves without the other. Hands that are too tight or too loose can destroy a golf swing. It is excessive use of the hands that turns the clubface off line, more often than not.

The hands should be firm but free—there is a fine line—and not coming in cocked and staying cocked in the downswing. If the left elbow stays close to your body and if the left hip out-turns the left arm, you've allowed the forearm and hands to come in front of you, and that will put your hands at finish between your head and left shoulder. You will get a more upright finish rather than a flat finish. Your divot will probably be six to eight inches long.

In practicing to keep the elbows in close, it is recommended that you use an iron, as there is always a tendency to swing harder and try to hit a longer ball with a wood. As you get the feeling of the elbows in close, then try it with the woods.

In summation, remember that it is a body hit—not a hand hit.

percentage
golf

26

by *Gary McCord*

Many golfers are familiar with the 16th hole at Cypress Point in Monterey, California, but for those who aren't, it's a par-3 hole which demands a carry of over 200 yards across Pacific Ocean and some jagged rocks to a relatively small green protected by four bunkers. It's a gorgeous hole and an architect's dream, but it sure doesn't always play like a dream.

To go after par, you've got to take chances. Most of the time, the wind is blowing—and it blows very hard from any direction in a matter of seconds.

You can play the hole in one of two ways: go for the pin and hope for the best or hit to an area short of the green and wide to the left and play the hole as an easy par-4 and try for a "bird." When the wind is blowing, the majority of players, including some pros, take the latter route. It's not too smart to take the par-3 route when the wind is blowing, especially from the side.

Playing this hole the "easy" way is playing percentage. If you go for the pin when the elements are against you and end up in

153

the ocean, the chances are good that you'll end up with a six and at best a five. But by playing it safe, there's a very good chance you'll get a three and no worse than a four.

There is much to say both for and against playing the percentages or playing it safe, especially if you're striving to break par. But this fact remains: you must size up a hole—the entire situation—and decide on a shot consistent with your talent. It's not too smart just to swing away and take the shortest route. You must plan your attack.

Golf course designers are a strange breed. They delight in punishing the errant player, the unthinking player, and rewarding the player who demonstrates skill and an intelligent approach. To put it another way, they delight in challenging your knowledge of the percentages of golf as well as the strokes.

Consider the 17th hole on the Whitemarsh course, where the Philadelphia Open often is played. It's a short par-5 with a water hazard bisecting the fairway 25 yards in front of the green. Golfers like Nicklaus can reach it in two. But how many golfers can hit like Nicklaus—even among the pros now playing the tour? Yet most of the players who face this challenge see it as that. They go for the green with their second shot, hoping for a birdie. The result, of course, is that many wind up in the water hazard or nearby sand and end up with a bogie or even worse. They would be wise to lay up to the hazard with their second shot and pitch to the green for an easy par and a possible bird.

Another example is the 18th hole at Laurel Valley, home of Arnie Palmer. It's a long par-4 with a lake to the right of a narrow fairway and in front of the green, which is off to the right from the golfer's view. How many golfers should go for the green on their second shot on a hole like this? The second shot is a long iron shot or maybe a wood. Again, if they fail to hit the shot perfectly, they're sure of a bogie and maybe worse. But a relatively "safe" shot along the fairway route, short of the green, means that a chip shot could possibly achieve par and no worse than a five.

Each hole demands thought, not only for approach but in use of clubs. A common mistake of a great many golfers—even some pros—is to use a driver on just about every tee, excepting the par-3s. They just think it's a must, the expected shot, to use a driver when they tee up the ball. They don't consider that another wood—or even an iron—might be the best for a particular hole or particular situation.

There's obviously no need to use a driver on a hole that measures considerably less than 400 yards if there's trouble near the spot where an average drive can be expected to land. Often a shorter hit will eliminate the chances of getting in trouble.

Consider this example: a short par-4 with an enormous bunker, the width of a fairway, covering all of the area from 50 yards out to the fringe of the green. A well-hit drive by even a non-pro can go into the sand on this Arizona hole. Yet most of the golfers who play this course, including some good ones, hit with a driver, hoping that the shot will land just short of the gaping bunker and set up a pitch of about 60 yards. How much more clever it would be if the players hit from the tee with a shorter wood or even an iron and then hit to the green with a 7- or 8-iron.

You must make yourself use the club that will get you in the best position for the next shot without taking great chances.

Many holes feature a slope going down to the green. A solid drive will leave the ball on the downward side and ensure a bad lie or a difficult shot. It would be percentage golf to play the shot short of the peak of the hill and ensure a good lie to hit to the green, even though the distance will be greater.

Few golfers, too, pay attention to the slope of a particular green. It is often pointed out that it's easier to make putts if you're stroking uphill rather than downhill. Yet many golfers will just hit directly at the waving flag and often roll past it or hit too long. Shots to a green that has a slope going upward, away from the golfer, should be played short to give the golfer the advantage of the upslope when he putts for a birdie.

But there are hundreds of examples of "percentage" golf. And usually there's a way to play each hole that can help the player.

Naturally, there are times when "gambling" is the only way to play a hole. If you *must* have a birdie to win an event, it's possible that you *must* take a gamble. If you are hitting your woods exceptionally well on a particular day, it's possible that a gamble—cutting a dogleg, hitting over water or over a tree—will be wholly in order and even "percentage."

Ben Hogan never gambled on a shot without reason. Before each event, he studied the course and learned its dangers, then played with knowledge. If a gamble was needed, the element of risk was a great deal less than for players who hadn't studied the course. Hogan knew the course he was playing on, and he knew his game and what he could do.

An excellent rule for all golfers to follow—except, of course, in very unusual situations—is to play the shot you know you can play while reducing risk. Don't play a shot that demands that the next will be the best you ever made.

One final note: there's a strong temptation to gamble on a shot that follows a shot that was terribly misplayed. Decline the temptation. Consider the odds against a "great" shot following a bad shot.

Use judgment on the course. Play the percentage the majority of the time.

physical conditioning

by *Grier Jones*

Once a golfer has established sound basic mechanics and tactics, physical condition often plays an important role in the kind of round he'll play; fatigue is a big factor in pressing, and hence a big factor in scoring, too. Yet a great percentage of golfers, including some pros, refuse to believe in exercise programs, good eating habits, and the necessity to rest at regular intervals. When it comes to keeping their bodies in shape, golfers, as a group, are notoriously ill-conditioned. They certainly can't compare in the physical department with other athletes, like baseball players, football players, trackmen, and swimmers.

Most serious athletes condition their bodies, exercise regularly, and eat properly throughout the year. But golfers generally dismiss the need for physical conditioning. They walk the appointed rounds and hit practice balls before a round, and that's it. A number of pros, however, have adopted exercise programs, even tennis, in order to compete on an equal footing with the stronger golfers.

Gary Player has always been a fitness nut, specializing in barbell exercises. He attributes his success completely to such exercises. His ability to beat the world's best in the Tournament of Champions is a tribute to his program.

It doesn't matter whether you're an amateur golfer playing once a week or a professional linksman playing every day. Physical well-being is a necessary ingredient to good golf. All the ability you have developed can be used best by a well-conditioned body.

Most golfers usually feel good when starting a round, but many are worn out after nine holes or a few more, and it shows in their games. Similarly, some golfers start out poorly and don't have the stamina or alertness they need to improve and salvage a round.

The value of excellent physical condition is continually evident in amateur and professional events. The top-flight players are usually in shape, well-conditioned, and able to "charge" while the poorer players or also-rans are in questionable condition. Put another way, the players who are obviously in questionable condition usually don't charge.

A major problem with many players is excess weight. Obesity, so prevalent in this age, is bad for anyone, golfer or non-golfer. It restricts the actions of any person, regardless of his task, and affects the game of a golfer noticeably.

Most people who follow tournament golf remember the impressive play of Billy Casper when he lost some weight, and his noticeable slipping when he regained weight. And Casper will agree, in all probability, that weight was to blame when he slipped. The "edge" is missing when you add on pounds. Bob Lunn became noticeably stronger after losing weight. There are many such examples of evident improvement after losing weight. Just look at the recent record of Jack Nicklaus after he slimmed down a few years ago.

Admittedly, some players who are obviously bulky can play very well—but more often than not they are simply big and poorly conditioned, and could play better still if they were in shape.

Without any doubt, the primary need of a good golfer is strong legs. In baseball, there's a saying that you're as strong as your legs. It also applies to golf. The legs are the key to distance and the ability to withstand the rigors of play, day after day. Distance results from the turn of the body, and the body is turned by the legs. So the

158

stronger the legs, the faster the turn and the harder you can hit the ball.

It is not my desire to prescribe an exercise program. Nearly everyone knows about exercises designed to increase the strength in the legs. Simple exercises such as skipping rope and jogging are great. Hand and wrist exercises should also be done, as well as swinging an overweight club. (Some pros swing a steel pipe.) But most of all, running is good. Running ensures a plentiful supply of oxygen in the blood, causes an improvement in body circulation, and builds up the muscles of the heart.

All golfers go stale on occasion. And many of them—especially amateurs who play a lot and the active professionals—think that the constant pressure and constant practice are causes of the staleness. They could be, of course. But it's more than probable that lack of conditioning is the real culprit, at least much of the time. If you're tired and run down, you can't play well or stay mentally alert.

But exercise alone is not the answer to physical woes. Good eating habits and adequate rest are also required. Admittedly, it's difficult for a tour golfer always to eat properly and eat on time. And sometimes it's difficult for other golfers too. But it's not impossible. And there is no excuse for inadequate rest.

In summary, I would say, exercise daily, eat as regularly as possible, and get plenty of rest, and you're sure to improve your game. You can prove this point for yourself just by studying the golfers who are riding the crest.

The Contributors

DALE ANDREASON: Head professional at Big Tee Golf Center, Buena Park, Calif.; veteran instructor and Tour player; winner of the Stockton Open, Santa Anita Open and many other events; holder of six course records.

DEANE BEMAN: Tour player since 1967; winner of six Tour events and numerous other tournaments; U.S. and British Amateur Champion; member of five Walker Cup teams and four Americas Cup squads.

RAFE BOTTS: Golf instructor associated with Griffith Park Golf Course, Los Angeles, Calif.; veteran Tour player; leading money winner on Canadian Tour.

MORTIE DUTRA: Head professional at Oakmont Country Club, Glendale, Calif.; veteran instructor and Tour player; winner of the Walter Hagen Invitational and numerous other events, including the PGA World Senior.

ZELL EATON: Head professional at Westward Ho Country Club, Indio, Calif.; instructor and Tour player for many years; winner of the California Open, Santa Anita Open, Montebello Open and other events.

DON FAIRFIELD: Director of Golf at Eldorado Country Club, Palm Desert, Calif.; longtime instructor and Tour player; winner of the Pensacola Open, St. Paul Open, Oklahoma City Open and many other events.

JIM FERRIER: Veteran Tour player; winner of the PGA Championship, Canadian Open and numerous other events; top 10 money winner six straight years.

JACK FLECK: Director of Golf at Plumas Lake Golf & Country Club, Marysville, Calif.; instructor and Tour player; winner of the U.S. Open, Texas Open, Bakersfield Open, the Illinois PGA Championship and many other events.

RALPH GULDAHL: Head professional at Braemar Country Club, Tarzana, Calif.; veteran instructor and Tour player; winner of the U.S. Open (two times), Masters Championship and 11 other Tour events; member of the PGA Hall of Fame and the American Golf Hall of Fame.

LABRON HARRIS: Tour player since 1964; winner of the Robinson Open and numerous other events. U.S. Amateur Champion.

BOB HARRISON: Head professional at Brentwood Country Club, Los Angeles, Calif.; instructor and Tour player; holder of the PGA driving record; winner of many events.

MAC HUNTER SR.: Head professional at Riviera Country Club, Pacific Palisades, Calif.; instructor and Tour player; winner of numerous events, including the Santa Anita Open; National Amateur Champion of Mexico.

JIM JAMIESON: Tour player since 1968; winner of the Western Open and numerous sectional events; $100,000 Tour winner in 1972.

GRIER JONES: Tour player since 1968; winner of Hawaiian Open and three other Tour events; NCAA Champion.

JOHN MAHAFFEY: Tour player since 1971; winner of the NCAA Championship and several regional events.

GARY McCORD: Leading money winner of the National Tournament Golf Association and Western Tournament Golf Association; NCAA College Division champion; winner of many regional events.

ERIC MONTI: Head professional at Hillcrest Country Club, Los Angeles, Calif; longtime instructor and Tour player; winner of three Tour events and numerous sectional events.

DAN MURPHY: Golf Director at Dorado Beach Country Club, Dorado, Puerto Rico; winner of many events and representative of Puerto Rico in the World Cup.

BILL OGDEN: Head professional at North Shore Country Club, Glenview, Ill.; instructor and Tour player, winner of many events, including the Illinois PGA Championship; Player of the Year (five times) in Illinois.

JIMMY POWELL: Head professional at Via Verde Country Club, San Dimas, Calif.; instructor and Tour player; Southern California PGA champion and winner of many tournaments.

MIKE SMITH: Director of Golf at Acapulco Princess Golf & Resort Hotel, Acapulco, Mexico; instructor and Caribbean Tour player; winner of many events in the United States and the Bahamas.

RON TAYLOR: Director of Golf at Azusa Greens Country Club, Azusa, Calif.; instructor and winner of many sectional events.

ELLSWORTH VINES: Head professional at LaQuinta Country Club, Palm Desert, Calif.; veteran instructor and Tour player; winner of numerous events.

HENRY WILLIAMS: Head professional at Berkleigh Country Club, Fleetwood, Pa.; veteran instructor and Tour player; winner of the Tucson Open, Jamaica Open and numerous sectional events.